NEXT

PRAISE FOR *NEXT*

With every assignment there is always a "next." Mike Tedder, my friend and co-laborer for the Kingdom, has captured the secret of living in the now and moving forward into the Next. It is too easy to trip ourselves up, getting stuck when we follow our own way. But Next never looks back. Next always causes us to leave our now, and Mike boldly challenges us to "leave it and let it go!" It is only through being free to follow God's call that He can lead us into the Kingdom and all He has for us. Thank you, Mike for using this opportunity to lead us on to the path of faith as we follow in the light and steps of our Lord. You have always been an encourager and support. You have held the arms of many who were growing tired. *Next* will be as the rock on which Aaron and Hur supported the arms of Moses, so that he could move forward into Next.

~**Malcolm Burleigh,** executive director,
Assemblies of God, US Missions
and author of *Assignment Led, or Agenda Driven?*

Mike Tedder is a pastor of pastors and a leader of leaders. In his book, *NEXT,* Mike will help guide us through life's most difficult question: "What is God's plan for my life?" Every reader will find *NEXT* both encouraging and helpful for their spiritual journey.

~**Aaron Burke,** lead pastor, Radiant Church, Tampa, FL

One of the amazing things about God is this: he's never stuck; he's never stagnant, and he's never stationary. Even in seasons when we feel trapped or contained, we can find peace in that moment. Why? Because God has our NEXT in place NOW! My friend, Pastor Mike Tedder, has written an amazing book that will empower and equip you with the necessary tools to recognize and seize your NEXT NOW!

~**Jim Raley,** apostle, pastor, evangelist,
Calvary Christian Center, Ormond Beach, FL,
and author of *Hell's Spells* and *Dream Killers*

Where we are in life and ministry is extremely important. However, where we are going next is just as important. How can we know where "Next" is, or how to prepare for the journey, or how to take the journey, or how to recognize the place when we arrive? My friend Mike Tedder, lead pastor of the Tabernacle Church in Atlanta, provides valuable, practical, and experience-tested answers to these questions. Pastor Tedder generously shares his hard-earned knowledge, savviness, and expertise in the pages of *NEXT: Discovering & Following God's Path & Pace for Your Life.* Mike's book will help you. Read it. It will not only help you get to your "Next". It will make you better on the trip and more effective when you get there!

~**Dr. Terry Raburn,** superintendent,
Peninsular Florida Assemblies of God

In my good friend Mike Tedder's first book, he writes about putting one's complete trust in the Lord's plan for our lives. There are those who spend their days worried to no end, concerned about things they have no control over—namely, tomorrow. As you read the words of *NEXT*, you will sense the calm, abiding presence of our Lord come near, as your faith builds knowing that God has your NEXT!

~**Rich Wilkerson,** lead pastor, evangelist,
Trinity Church Miami, FL

I love *NEXT*! This is probably one of the most needed messages for the day we live in. It is a road map for your destiny! The new book, *NEXT,* by friend, pastor, and author Mike Tedder is a book written for those ready to defeat lethargy, confusion, and fear. Those are three attack methods of the enemy to stop God's anointed sons and daughters from ever accomplishing their destiny. *NEXT* is a wake-up call from heaven that now is the *kairos,* God-appointed time to take control of your destiny. In his book, Mike calls all of us into accountability for what we are called to do! Are you ready to dream again? Then start this book today! No more excuses! God is getting you ready! One of my favorite verses is in 1 Peter 4:12–13 (MSG): "Friends, when life gets really difficult, don't jump to the conclusion that God isn't on the job. Instead, be glad that you are in the very thick of what Christ experienced. This is a spiritual refining process, with glory just around the corner" verses No more waiting! Grab your next! Glory awaits you!

~**Pat Schatzline,** author, evangelist,
& CEO, Remnant Ministries International

If you care deeply about your ministry and you're seeking your "NEXT" season, then put *NEXT* on your required reading list. You will learn to identify what is keeping you from moving forward with this Spirit-led guide to eliminating obstacles and stepping boldly into what God has for you.

~**Rev. John Dougherty,** superintendent,
Georgia Assemblies of God

Without a doubt, *NEXT* addresses a very common issue among Christians of all ages today. For many Christians, the Christian highway to eternity is a vague and difficult pathway, which is difficult to discern. Rev. Mike Tedder, however, lays out a systematic plan to move along the pathway, which is relevant and scriptural. His title not only raises the curiosity of the average Christian but the text is very easy to engage and follow. Most importantly, it is also relevant and down-to-earth. The book has the potential to provide a realistic roadmap for Christians who desire to grow spiritually and press toward the mark of the high calling in Jesus Christ. I believe it would be suitable reading for teenagers and adults. It certainly has a place in Christian literature in the twenty-first century.

~**LTC Emanuel Williams,** retired chaplain,
Assemblies of God Staff Pastor Tabernacle Church

Everyone has a NEXT! At no point in life are we stuck without hope. We are trapped by neither our successes nor our failures. In his book, *NEXT,* Mike Tedder teaches us these lessons and so many more. He does an excellent job laying out a path for life's transforming transitions.

~Duke Matlock, executive coach,
president at Invest Leadership Initiative

NEXT

DISCOVERING & FOLLOWING GOD'S PATH and PACE for Your LIFE

MIKE TEDDER

NASHVILLE

NEW YORK • LONDON • MELBOURNE • VANCOUVER

NEXT

Discovering & Following God's Path and Pace for Your Life

Published in New York, New York, by Morgan James Publishing. Morgan James is a trademark of Morgan James, LLC. www.MorganJamesPublishing.com

Proudly distributed by Ingram Publisher Services.

Morgan James BOGO™

A **FREE** ebook edition is available for you or a friend with the purchase of this print book.

CLEARLY SIGN YOUR NAME ABOVE

Instructions to claim your free ebook edition:
1. Visit MorganJamesBOGO.com
2. Sign your name CLEARLY in the space above
3. Complete the form and submit a photo of this entire page
4. You or your friend can download the ebook to your preferred device

ISBN 9781636980287 paperback
ISBN 9781636980294 ebook
Library of Congress Control Number:
2022943841

Cover & Interior Design by:
Christopher Kirk
www.GFSstudio.com

Morgan James PUBLISHING Builds *with...* Habitat for Humanity Peninsula and Greater Williamsburg

Morgan James is a proud partner of Habitat for Humanity Peninsula and Greater Williamsburg. Partners in building since 2006.

Get involved today! Visit MorganJamesPublishing.com/giving-back

To my wife, Jeannie, I love you!
Thank you for taking this journey in life with me.
Thank you for embracing each Next that God has given us.
We have learned and are learning
that God really does have our Nexts.
You are God's gift as a fabulous wife,
an incredible mother, and an amazing Mimi.

CONTENTS

ACKNOWLEDGMENTS

I n this, my first book writing project, I had no idea what to expect. Throughout this journey, there have been many helpful and encouraging people who supported the process. Thank you to all who believe in me.

To my wife, Jeannie, and my children, Candace and Aaron, Andrew and Brianna, and Caleb and Melissa, and all of my grandchildren, thank you for loving me. Your lives drive me to write to leave a legacy for you. Your encouragement to finish this book was so helpful. Your support in our life of ministry is humbling. Your growth in this journey of "Nexts" is amazing to watch. I love you!

Thank you, Mom! Your patience, grace, love, and kindness are unparalleled. You started me on so many Nexts and then encouraged me through them all. You never gave up on me, even when I'm sure I tested your resolve. I love you, Mom.

Thank you to my many ministry friends who have helped me find many of my Nexts with prayer, love, and friendship. Your kindness and grace empowered me, even when you did not know it. Thank you, Mike Escoe, David Santiago, Jim Raley, Duke Matlock, and Malcom Burleigh.

Thank you, Billy and Al, for revealing Jesus to me, discipling me, and encouraging me. I would not be on this journey with Jesus without you. You both diligently planted and watered, and God continues to give the increase.

Thank you, Cortney Donelson, my editor. I really do not know how you do it. Your work is amazing. In addition, your encouragement goes above and beyond what most would give.

Thank you, David Hancock and Morgan James Publishing, for giving me this opportunity to encourage many others on their journeys to Next. Your help in this new adventure keeps me moving and successful.

Introduction

THE GOD OF STEPS
AND DETAILS

As a teen, I was a gamer. I played a lot video games. You only have to do a Google search to discover the only game I ever owned as a teen and played at home: Pong. Pong was basically a black and white version of a table tennis or Ping-pong game. The other games I enjoyed sat nestled in arcades, game rooms, or convenience stores. Most often, you could have found me at the local convenience store, battling a pinball game or engrossed in Space Invaders or Centipede, which was my favorite game at one particular convenience store. I would often set the high score, sometimes erasing one of my earlier wins. Maybe it was the simplicity of the game that helped garner my success. One plastic ball to roll with your fingers to aim the gun and one button to push to fire, unlike many hand-held controllers today that sport multiple buttons on the top, sides, or bottom, which people must know how to maneuver.

The games cost me a quarter to play. That twenty-five-cent piece gave me three lives to use up before I'd see "Game Over" flash on the screen. Then I would deposit another quarter to play again.

The "gamer's code" was this: If you came to play a game that someone was already playing, you could place your quarter on the console and say, "I've got next." This would give you the privilege of playing the game immediately after the current player finished their active game. Sometimes, there would be a line of people waiting to play a game, which meant there was a line of quarters on the console too.

During a recent season of prayer, God reminded me of this "gaming" season in my life. He brought to my memory the gamer's code of "I've got next." As crazy as it sounds, I believe He spoke to me and said, *Mike, I put my quarter down on your life, and I've got next.* This shook me. I wondered, *why me?* What does God's quarter look like? What next?

I don't have the answers yet. And I don't believe I will ever be able to answer these questions without Him. I'm now on a journey to discover "Next." The lessons I've learned so far have been amazing, and I keep learning. At the encouragement of the Lord and my friends in my faith family who have heard me share about some of these lessons, I now share them with you. My prayer, as I write this, is that you will hear God as He puts His quarter on your life's console and says, *I've got* your *next.*

Let's begin with a powerful passage to which the Lord directed me as I explored "Next."

> *The Lord directs the steps of the godly. He delights in every detail of their lives. Though they stumble, they will never fall, for the Lord holds them by the hand* (Psalm 37:23–24).

The first consideration of this verse is that it refers to the godly or righteous. Let's be clear. I, like the apostle Paul, am chief among sinners. Left to myself, I am not righteous or godly. However, in His incredible grace and mercy, Jesus has made himself available to be my righteousness as I follow Him. With this understanding, we can move forward, knowing this verse reflects what my life and your life *can be.*

The promise of this passage is powerful. The one who directs is the Lord—not an angel, a minister, a prophet, an evangelist, nor even a devil. It is amazing to me that God himself would be so involved in my life to direct me. Doesn't He know there are close to eight billion people on earth? Yet repeatedly, He says that He chose each one of us. Does he not know that I am one of the chief sinners? Well, yes, He does, and He chose me anyway. It's His choosing, His love, that empowers me so that I am no longer ruled by sin or wrongdoing.

He chooses all of us and directs our steps.

God directs every step, every detail, every day. Can we truly process this phenomenon? In one day—to stay healthy—I average over 10,000 steps. And God is directing each one. He is involved in every detail of my life. Yours too. I don't even know how many daily details are in an average life. I know it's a mind-boggling number.

I have a personal goal to live one hundred years before I am promoted to my ultimate "Next." Having become a Christ-follower and disciple around my seventeenth birthday means God has had at least 30,295 days to direct my 10,000-plus steps. This equals roughly 302,950,000 steps and infinitely more details—just for my life alone. Now, if we add in all the Christ-followers around the globe, all those who have lived in each generation, well . . . it's an astronomical number of steps and details to think about. This just validates how big God really is.

So does His directing our steps mean we never get out of step or stumble? The psalmist who wrote the thirty-seventh Psalm shined some light on this question: *The righteous may stumble, and the hand of God will steady them.* Even as He directs our steps, we are still the ones taking them. We are not puppets. We can—and will—stumble or get off course. However, He is not an absentee director. The Holy Spirit, God's spirit, is with us always. He will steady us during every stumble or misstep. This concept of His grace—with us always, reaching to steady us—may be a different perception or understanding of God than what you already have. If it is,

I encourage you to continue to read as we look at the lives of Moses and others in the Bible to see just how God directs people to their Nexts.

The psalmist penned these words in Psalm 119:105: "Your word is a lamp to guide my feet and a light for my path." In my quest to know God, I have tried hard to live with integrity, using His Word, the Bible, as a guide. I work and study to show myself approved. I also recognize I am not a scholar in the genuine sense of the term. I have deeply rooted values when it comes to the use of the Word. One of the most significant of those values is that I do not want to be someone who just hears or even knows the Word; I want to be a *doer of the Word*. This is a lifelong journey.

I am thankful for the psalmist's words in Psalm 119. His Word is a lamp and light to my feet and path. So if God is directing those 302,950,000-plus steps over my lifetime, it never has to be in the dark. If I do stumble or misstep, it does not have to be because of any darkness. His Word is the lamp and light. How incredibly important it is to me to read the Word daily—sometimes multiple times every day. This keeps the light and lamp shining brightly.

Another option is to own a Bible and not read it. Then, it's like having a flashlight and not flipping it on, having lights in your house or office and not turning them on, having lights on your car and not using them at night, or having a match and never striking it. You get the picture. When we read the Word, it will not return empty or void. Yes, even in rote, daily reading plans, God can light up your life. Be creative: read it, sing it, memorize it, study it, discuss it; journal it, S.O.A.P. it (for all you note takers and goal setters) . . . just do it!

It will light up your life!

1
LET'S GO BEGINS WITH LET GO

To get to our Next, we have to let go of what is keeping us from moving.

God's got your Next!

God has poured His love on our lives, and that love says He's got our "Next." Every Next that God's got will be better than any Next we can manufacture. Let's look at Moses's journey.

Exodus 2:11–15: *Many years later, when Moses had grown up, he went out to visit his own people, the Hebrews, and he saw how hard they were forced to work. During his visit, he saw an Egyptian beating one of his fellow Hebrews. After looking in all directions to make sure no one was watching, Moses killed the Egyptian and hid the body in the sand. The next day, when Moses went out to visit his people again, he saw two Hebrew men fighting. "Why are you beating up your friend?" Moses said to the one who had started the fight. The man replied, "Who appointed you to be our prince and judge? Are you going to kill me as you killed that Egyptian yesterday?" Then Moses was afraid, thinking, "Everyone knows what I did." And sure enough, Pharaoh heard what had happened, and he tried to kill Moses. But Moses fled from Pharaoh and went to live in the land of Midian.*

The story continues in Exodus 3: 7–10:

*Then the Lord told him, "I have certainly seen the oppression of my people in Egypt. I have heard their cries of distress because of their harsh slave drivers. Yes, I am aware of their suffering. So I have come down to rescue them from the power of the Egyptians and lead them out of Egypt into their own fertile and spacious land. It is a land flowing with milk and honey . . . Look! The cry of the people of Israel has reached me, and I have seen how harshly the Egyptians abuse them. **Now go, for I am sending you** to Pharaoh. You must lead my people Israel out of Egypt* (emphasis mine).

To get to our Next, we have to let go of our "used to be" and perhaps our "is now." *Then Moses was afraid, thinking, "Everyone knows what I did."* Moses's fear controlled his thinking. There were no cell phones, house phones, or office phones; no internet, email, social media, or computers; no newspapers, radio, or television news. In Moses's day, the only way for news to spread was from person to person. It would have been unrealistic to believe that "everyone knows." As is often the case with any of us, Moses's fear had manipulated his thinking. Yes, he had stepped out of line. Yes, he took matters into his own hands. Yes, he was raised in Pharoah's court. And yes, he was an Israeli. One who had killed someone while trying to do what he thought was right. He had perhaps acted in his sense of destiny but likely not in God's direction. Moses was fighting for his family. He tried to be secretive, looking to see if anyone was watching, and then burying the body in the sand. Yes, yes, yes. Even when you add up all the yeses, it would be virtually impossible to believe that roughly one million Israelis and countless Egyptians had all heard what he had done by *the next day.*

We can't think straight, right, or objectively when our emotions are in control. Our perception becomes skewed. This is one reason the Bible says not to trust the emotions in your heart—contrary to what most love ballads and country songs instruct. Proverbs 28:26 teaches, "Those who trust their own insight are foolish . . ."

The heart is the storage compartment for many things, including our emotions. Our emotions, such as fear, cannot be trusted and often make us act foolishly. We must guard our hearts. We must guard our reactions to our emotions. After all, emotions do have purpose. But their purpose has never been to rule our lives; that is not why God designed them.

When our perspectives are skewed because of fear, we think our pasts are too awful for God to use us now. Moses's fear caused him to run. And he ran far. He hid. It appears he did not intend to return to his family in Egypt. It seems he never intended to make things right. His fear did not just dominate that one moment; it was so large that it dominated his life. His fear dominated his past, present, and future. The psalmist had not written these words when Moses ran away, but the character of God was ever-present: "He has removed our sins as far from us as the east is from the west" (Psalm 103:12).

Rather than trust our emotions, we should trust the King of our hearts. We must work daily at checking in with and submitting everything, including our emotions, to Him.

Let me share with you one of my favorite passages for managing the emotion of fear.

*But now, O Jacob, listen to the Lord who created you. O Israel, the one who formed you says, "**Do not be afraid**, for I have ransomed you. I have called you by name; you are mine. . . . When you go through deep waters, I will be with you. When you go through rivers of difficulty, you will not drown. When you walk through the fire of oppression, you will not be burned up; the flames will not consume you. For I am the Lord, your*

*God, the Holy One of Israel, your Savior . . . because you are precious to me. You are honored, and I love you. **Do not be afraid**, for I am with you . . ."* (Isaiah 43:1–5, emphasis mine).

Isaiah reminds us it is never a matter of *if* we will face waters, rivers, and fire. It is a matter of *when* we will face them. We do not have to fear because God will direct our steps as we pass through the waters and rivers and walk through the fire. He is the Lord, our God!

We should learn from our past but not live in it. Moses seemed to have a sense of his destiny. When we have a sense of our destiny, it is easy to try to manufacture our Nexts. We know God has a plan and is planning to use us, so we step out. The caution we must consider is that if He did not direct the steps, if He did not light up particular paths with His lamp, then we are wandering in the dark. This could be one reason God used the incredible illustration of a burning bush that never burned up to speak to Moses in his hiding place. I certainly cannot speak for Moses, but it seems easy to look back and learn. Moses did not have the verses in Psalms to read. He did not have arcade games and quarters. What he did have was a burning bush, and God engaged with Moses in the first of many direct conversations with him.

Moses learned that destiny must wait on direction. Next steps are crucial to the fulfillment of destiny. Moses's manufactured action and his subsequent fear led him on a detoured journey of steps through a desert for forty years.

Know this: If your sense of destiny is God-given, He will find you—even on the backside of a desert. He will take you by the hand and steady you. He will light up your path. He will lead you to and through your destiny and your destination. He sees you where you are. And He still chooses you. He's coming for you. He's got you. *He's got your Next.*

MOVING DAY

To get to our Next, we have to move away from our *now.*

In Exodus 3:8–10, God speaks to Moses from the burning bush. In verse 9, the Lord told him " Look! The cry of the people of Israel has reached me, and I have seen how harshly the Egyptians abuse them. *Now go, for I am sending you . . .*" (italics mine).

The laws of science dictate that we cannot stay in the same place and move forward at the same time. It is physically impossible. If I am sitting in my favorite chair, I cannot go anywhere else unless I leave where I am. I realize this is an obvious truth. However, I still feel amazed when I listen to people who describe their desire to go somewhere new and yet have not moved from where they are to investigate or prepare for anything new. We can think about moving—meditate on it, talk about it, dream about it, debate it, discuss it—or even pray about it, but until we get up and move, we won't go anywhere. Moving forward into our Next will always require us to leave our *now.* Whatever our now is, we will have to walk away from it.

For Moses, his now was a comfortable and thriving family business. He was a successful shepherd with a large herd. He had established distance from his past, the castle and the king's-court life. Moses had made a successful transition into his new life. For forty years, he had grown his business and family, becoming an inspiration to all in the region. Why would anyone want to leave that?

Moses would discover it would not be easy. He would have to reckon with leaving all he had to go to the unknown. And by the way, the challenge to leave it all, his now, was coming from a voice in a burning bush. Yes, it was God's voice, but think about it: He's on the backside of the wilderness when a bush on fire (but not burning up) speaks to him. And this bush tells him to leave his now to go back to a place that remembers his past—including all of his failures. To a place where he might be wanted for murder. Well, it was God speaking, and the call to Moses was to follow the Lord's Next, which required him to leave his now. What about you?

It's too easy to sit in our nows while celebrating our successes, even worrying over our failures. I appreciate coaches who lead teams to higher levels of success, including multiple championships over years. Often, you hear the coaches speak about how they celebrate their successes in short bursts. They often say, "We will celebrate our success today and tomorrow, maybe for this week, but then it's back to work for the next game (or season)." They teach players to learn from their failures but to move on from them. In sports, it's said players and coaches must have short memories regarding failures. Learn the lesson and then move on to the next opportunity for success.

The truth is, both success and failure have a way of keeping hold of us. To get to our Nexts, we have to be free.

People often say, "Be careful what you pray for." It's true, meaning—in this book—if you're not willing to move with God, perhaps the first prayer should be for a heart transformation and submission to God's will . . . for His Next for your life. We want God to do supernatural works in and for us. When He does works like this in His people, they are usually moving, leaving their nows behind. Moses saw the snake only after he threw the shepherd's staff to the ground. He saw the snake turn back into the shepherd's staff only after he picked the snake up by the tail. He saw his hand become diseased only after he put it in his coat and pulled it back out. He saw the return of health in his hand only after he put it in his coat again and pulled it out again. He saw the response of the people only after he told them through Aaron what God had said. He saw all ten plagues come upon Egypt only after he went to Pharoah and told him what God had said. He saw the deliverance of Israel only after he left his now and obediently went to Egypt. We have to be willing to let go of our nows and move with God if we are going to ask God to move in and for us.

Changing from our nows to our Nexts is often challenging. We know our nows. We don't always know what our Nexts are. Even if we know what they are, we may not know what the journey is like to get there. God loves the journey as much as—if not more than—the destination itself. It's in the journey from our nows to our Nexts where He grows us, develops us, disciples us, equips us, and empowers us. We can work with the change or the change will work us.

Embrace the journey as you release your now to travel to your Next.

IN GOD, WE TRUST

To get to our Next, we have to trust that God's got our Nexts! Remember that video game that cost a quarter to play? If you looked at every quarter that lined those consoles—and every quarter in your car's spare change compartment—you would find the same phrase: *In God We Trust*. I have resolved in my life to not let a quarter trust God more than me. When we put the quarter in the video game machine, we trusted we would get the next game. When we trust God with our Nexts, we will get exactly what He has promised us.

In the Exodus passages we explored earlier, it is recorded, "The next day . . . But Moses fled from . . ." Moses's first "Next day" in this story did not go so well. He fled. He ran. He hid. He did not have this book to read to know to trust God more than a quarter seems to trust Him. Though Moses had not yet experienced the burning bush, he still had some sense of his destiny to help the Israelites. And after he tried to help with the *wrong* action, he could not trust God.

That is how many of us feel when we do the right thing the wrong way. When I made my second ministry move as a youth pastor, I did it with the right *intent* of following God and His plan for my life. However, I did not make the choice the right *way*. In my frustration, I jumped at an opportunity without doing my due diligence or trusting God to give me my Next. The result was my shortest tenure in ministry—about five months. After that tenure, I returned to Bible college through doors God opened to get me where He wanted me to go. Ironically, the church I left to go on my five-month journey offered me the opportunity to serve with them for a second tenure with more responsibility and compensation. I learned through this journey to trust God, even in my frustrations and unsettling moments. I learned to trust God's grace even when I make choices apart from His plan. I learned He does not give up on me like others do, including myself.

Maybe this will help you trust God with your Next. We don't have to create our Nexts! We just have to follow the steps and path God directs us to and lights up for us. We can be thankful that all we have to do is follow His direction. He takes care of creating our Nexts and equipping us for them. By the way, if God can create the universe and all that's in it, including the entire world in six days, then our Nexts should not be that difficult for Him. I mean, if He can create our human bodies out of the dirt with thirteen intricate systems all working together, then creating our Nexts is very doable for Him.

Sometimes, it's difficult for us to let Him create our Nexts because we want to do it. We should take caution here. When we create our own Nexts, it can be just as detrimental as Moses's self-created Next. Moses's Next encompassed murder, running away, living in hiding, cutting himself off from family and friends, and starting over with nothing when he could have had everything. Take it from Moses; when we create our own Nexts, it usually does not end well.

How can we develop our "In God, we trust" quotient? Spend time with God. Listen in prayer and read the Word! If we are asking God for our Next, then we should be quiet and listen for His direction. This can come through the inspired words of the Bible, which, remember, are collectively the light and lamp to our feet and path. It can come in the "still small voice" as God speaks to us in our intimate times of prayer. God does not play hide-and-seek with His plan or will for your life. If we are asking Him for Next and remain quiet so we can hear Him speak, He will share. It could be an impression or thought we have as we listen. Or it could be an audible voice—at least audible to our spiritual ears. All these impressions, thoughts, and words should be filtered through the Bible. God is not the author of confusion. He brings clarity with His words.

To get to our Next, we have to let go of our used-to-be. We have to move away from our now, and we must trust that God's got our Next!

Yes, God's got your Next because it's a call from Him.

2

THE CALL TO OUR NEXTS

The divine call to our Next comes with need-to-know clarity.

All the Nexts you would ever have, God has got. That's interesting because some of us aren't interested in releasing our Nexts to Him. But, as we've discussed, God is keenly interested in every detail and every step.

Have you ever reached a place in your life and realized, "I don't know what's next?" Have you ever gotten to a place and said, "I'm scared about next"? Have you ever hit a point and said, "Oh boy, I don't know how to do what's next," "I don't know where next is," or "I don't know *what* next is!" Your question might be, *how many times have I been here?* I've been "there" many times, where I just don't know what Next is.

Let's consider the call to our Next. In Exodus, Chapter 3, Moses gets his call to his Next. He had already killed a guy when they tried conflict resolution. Then he ran away because he knew he shouldn't be killing anybody. He ran to the desert, married a girl, and worked for his new father-in-law. His father-in-law set Moses up in the business, and when the story picks up, for the past forty years, Moses has been in the desert doing business, serving as a successful shepherd. Then God speaks to him. And this is where God *calls* Moses to his Next.

Remember, Moses ran away for forty years. What we think is our running away may be God's education process. Forty years of education! This four-decade-long class is not mentioned in the Bible, but when you understand what shepherds learn about leadership, it's amazing. And so, let's call this Moses's forty years of *leadership* education. Moses had been raised in Pharoah's house (the king of Egypt's castle). He was given formal education from his childhood through young adulthood. He may have thought this time in the desert was a new life, a new time, a new season; but in reality, it was a new education.

Through the burning bush, the Lord intimates, "I have certainly seen the oppression of my people in Egypt. I have heard the cries of their distress because of their harsh slave drivers."

He's reminding Moses of where he came from, that he'd killed a slave driver, an Egyptian. *Yes, I am aware of their suffering. So I have come down.* (I'm paraphrasing a little here, but listen to what God had to say because Moses missed it.) *I have come down to rescue them from the power of the Egyptians and lead them out of Egypt to their own fertile and spacious land. It is a land flowing with milk and honey—the land where the Canaanites, Hittites, Amorites, Perizzites, Hivites, and Jebusites now live*. All the "Zite" families lived there. Then verse 9: "Look! The cry of the people of Israel has reached me." God says it again because He's connecting back to where he started: the crying of the people, the harsh slave drivers . . . these sights and sounds caused Moses to remember what he had done to leave Egypt because he feared for his life. Moses must have thought everybody would remember what he did. *The cry of the people of Israel has reached me, and I have seen how harshly the Egyptians have abused them*. Verse 10 is the call: "Now go, for I am sending you to Pharaoh . . ." This is the guy who wants revenge on Moses! Go back and read it. God is going to send Moses back to those who want to kill him: *You must lead my people Israel out of Egypt.*

The call to our Next will always find us where we are.

Let me tell you where Moses was. Moses was shepherding the flock of Jethro, his father-in-law's flock, to the far side of the desert. How do you know where the far side of the desert is? It's where you won't easily be found. It's on the backside of nowhere. Have you ever lived on the backside of nowhere? There's a place called Slapout, Alabama. A little community just south of Holtville, Alabama. I think the name came about because it's so far out. So Moses may have been in "Slapout" desert, tending to his sheep, near Horeb. There, the angel of the Lord appeared to him in flames of fire from within that bush. It's not common, but it would be feasible for a dried-up bush in the desert to catch fire and burn up. But Moses saw something different. The bush was on fire, it did not burn up.

When I start a fire at my fireplace, the logs I put in there burn up. I go to bed when the last piece burns. When I get up the next morning, there is nothing but ashes in that fireplace. But the bush that Moses saw was unique; it was not burning up. It just kept sizzling without being consumed. God had gotten his attention.

The call to our Next will find us where we are too. We could be on the backside of nowhere or somewhere else, perhaps in the throes of fame or success. God might find us at the base of some mountain or in the valley beside it. Regardless, He will speak to us. He will speak to us to get our attention. You don't have to go looking for your Next; you just have to pay attention when He shows up.

When someone says, "I've never heard from God," a big question mark erupts in my mind. From Genesis through Revelation, there's proof that God has always found people where they are. In fact, He says He pursues us. He chose us long before we ever choose Him. God may be knocking right now, and you're not answering. God may have been calling, but you haven't been listening. God may have been giving you signs, but you're not even looking. God will find you where you are, and when He finds you, He may communicate something you *ain't* expecting.

The call to our Next will be from Him.

The call to our Next will be from Him: capital 'H', the "Him." God wanted to make sure Moses understood this: "Do not come any closer, the Lord warned. Take off your sandals, for you are standing on holy ground. I am the God of your father—the God of Abraham, the God of Isaac, and the God of Jacob" (Exodus 3:5–6). When Moses heard this, he got it; he got that this was God. Moses covered his face because he was afraid to look at God.

At the bush, God orchestrates this encounter with Moses, and Moses covers his face in humility because he realizes the God of the universe is right there, speaking to him. The call to our Next will find us! The call to our Next will always be from Him!

If you're a Christ-follower—and even if you're not—God calls us to follow Him. Always look and ask, "Is this the Lord?" And if you're a Christ-follower, I promise you that nearly every time, it is the Lord, or you wouldn't be asking, "Is this the Lord?" You know it is! Often, we just don't want to do what He's communicating or asking.

Come on now! When people say, "I didn't know if it was the Lord," well, why not? Because it scares you? Then it is

God. Why? Because it's bigger than you? Then it is God. Why? Because it's something that you can't do by yourself? Then, it is God! Once we can validate that the call is from Him, we understand that the call from Him will get us where He wants us to go.

| **The call to our Next expects a response every time.**

"When the Lord saw Moses," verse 4, "coming to take a closer look, God called him from the middle of the bush, 'Moses! Moses!'" And Moses replied, "Here I am." God always wants you to be engaged. The moment that call to our Next comes, we need to respond to the Lord. Don't ignore Him anymore. I believe there are people that God has called, who have never, ever responded to Him. They've ignored Him. We may never be as brave or brash to stick our hands up and say, "Here I am!" but many of us have ignored Him.

Some people reason, *well, that's just the pastor talking. That was not God.* Let me help you with pastors, OK? There's a story in the Bible where God spoke through a jack-ass (King James Version language), and if God could speak through a jackass, He can speak through me, a pastor. Are you with me now?

You may say that I am wrong, and that's perfectly fine! I don't care, but when God uses a jackass to speak to us, we should respond. Look, if God will not use pastors, spiritually mature leaders, or others to speak into our lives, why does He have them here? Do you know what God calls people?

Sheep! Have you herded sheep? Pastors have to lead, care for, protect, and grow sheep. God most definitely uses pastors to speak to you. He will use His Word to speak to you. He'll write in the sky if necessary. He will whisper with His still, small voice into your ear so that you'll hear Him. He'll find ways to speak to you! You just have to pay attention and respond to Him when He does. Maybe start like Moses with something simple: *Here I am, Lord*. Mary said those words too. If you look at some other prominent Bible characters, you'll see their responses that allowed God to lead their lives.

The call to our Next will shake us up.

What's next? One reason we want to ignore a call to our Next is we know it will shake us up. Most calls from God shake us up. If He's calling us to a life of righteousness or holiness, it is in response to our sinful nature. It's easier to live sinfully than righteously. Right? Natural beings go toward sinful things. But when God calls us, He empowers us not to live sinfully. He empowers us to live righteously. Sometimes, we miss that because we want to live righteously on our own accord. That is just not possible.

Some people have been in church for a long time, trying to live righteously on their own and blowing it. The reason they're blowing it is that they're trying to do it on their own. God is the only one who can empower us to live righteously! Why? He *is* our righteousness! If we could live righteously on our own, listen to me, we could go back to the Old Testament and live by the law! Can't be done! Admittedly, in the Scripture, it can't be done! But what can be done is living with Jesus, who empowers us to live righteously.

The call to our Next doesn't just shake us up. Look at what happened to Moses. As soon as the call was issued, in verse 12, "But Moses protested to God . . ." Moses was all shook up! Moses didn't protest just once; he protested five times in a row.

We might believe we wouldn't protest God, but many of us simply ignore Him. Some may say, "I've never told God no," but you've never told Him yes, either. Maybe we never follow through with what He's put on our life. Maybe we never made it to the place He wants us to go. Maybe we never accomplish what He gave us to accomplish, and we've found all the reasons it won't work.

It is then that God says, "Hold on! That thing isn't what I called you to. I called you to me! Come to me, and I will take care of the rest. Just walk in faith." We've got to walk in faith.

Five times, Moses protested because he was shaken up. This is what I'm excited about! Even though Moses protested five times, God showed resiliency. Just so you understand resilience, it's the capacity to recover quickly from difficulties and toughness. God can respond to your protests. God can respond when you ignore Him, and God can respond when you don't listen, when you don't see, and when you don't hear. God can respond to you in the right way, and thank God He does! He could just say, "Pssshhh! You get what you get."

After all, that's what happened to Jeremiah. In Jeremiah Chapter 6, God tells the Israelites He is leaving them to their desires. History tells us how that ended: disastrous. From the fruit of our own schemes, when no offering or sacrifice is acceptable, God will let us do our own thing. But know this: He may have a new thing for you. God's got a Next thing in mind, and let me tell you what your Next is (not). It's never your own thing. Your Next is *His* thing.

When God calls you to your Next and it shakes you up, you have to listen, despite all uncertainties, to hear Him. Everybody's got uncertainty about something. Somebody tells us to do something for the first time, and we think *I don't know if I can do that.* In every new year, it seems everyone wants to do something new, and they make these crazy resolutions.

I'm going to resolve my finances.

I'm going to resolve to do my health better.

I'm going to resolve to go to the gym.

I'm going to invest in gyms every January and then by March, I'm selling out.

We must listen through our uncertainties to hear with clarity. Listen to the call again and see if you got what Moses missed. God had said to Him, "I have certainly seen the affliction of my people in Egypt. I have heard their cries and distress because of their harsh slave drivers, so, yes I have come down to rescue them from the power of the Egyptians and lead them out of Egypt into their own fertile, spacious land known as the land flowing with milk and honey." When God spoke of their afflictions and their distresses and the sufferings, He connected Moses through memory and passion to what had happened to him forty years ago. But did Moses miss the significance of this phrase? ". . . *so I have come down to rescue them.*" If Moses really *heard*—with ears to hear—what God had said and not just *listened* to what He said, I don't believe he would have ever protested.

The call to our Next often awakes our uncertainties.

Look what Moses said as he protested to God: "Who am I to appear before Pharaoh and who am I to lead the people of Israel out of Egypt?"

God answered, "I will be with you (He's already told him that) and this is your sign that I am the one who has sent you." How many of you know the sign? When you understand the sign, it will blow your mind. Listen to this: "When you would have brought the people out of Egypt, you will worship God on this very mountain." That's an incredible sign, what God told Moses.

The call to our Next *awakens our uncertainties*. You will doubt. You might ask things, such as:

- *Who am I to appear to?*
- *Who am I to lead?*
- *Who is this guy? (Meaning me.)*

I always thought that when I first came to Christ, I was a pimpled face, skinny, teenage kid, who was also a teen alcoholic, and God redeemed me. Then, six months after He redeemed me, He called me to ministry. I thought, *Who am I?* There were countless evangelists, pastors, missionaries—there are already all these people—why would He call me?

- *Who am I?*
- *I'm just an insignificant speck on the planet Earth. Even so, God would call me?*
- *Come on! I'm sure God's smarter than that!*

But God was resilient, and He kept calling until I understood. Until I relented. He just wants you to understand who is calling . . . and relent your Next to Him too.

God is our certainty.

With certainty, God answered the uncertainty of Moses when He said, "When you bring the people out of Egypt, you will worship God on this mountain, and I will be with you" (paraphrased). God left no doubt when He said He would be with Moses.

Moses already missed the first time God said He would come down to rescue the Israelites from the Egyptians, and then God promises to be with him. We think God is with missionaries; God is with pastors; God is with worship leaders, but we don't trust God is going to be with us in our layperson job. We won't believe God is going to be with us in our homes or in our neighborhoods.

God is going to be with you wherever you go! He said it: I will be with you! You may be on the backside of the desert, listening to sheep *bah* all day long, but let me tell you something. God's going to speak into your life, and God's going to be with you when you're on the backside of the desert, no matter which desert you find yourself in. God may even speak to you through a burning bush! Why not?

There's more. He wants you to know He's not just going to be with you in the bush, but He's going to be with you *every step* you take. How do we know? The steps of a righteous man (or woman) are ordered in the Lord!

Second, God said it was the sign! Just imagine how those words feel to your ears and heart. He didn't say, "You *might* worship me." He said, ". . . and you *will* worship me." That is a declarative statement—a done deal in God's eyes. You will worship me on this mountain where you are right now. But Moses wasn't on a mountain. He was on the far side of the desert. Not Horeb, not Sinai. If you read through the rest of Exodus, there comes a moment when they return to Sinai, and Moses goes to the top while who is at the bottom of Sinai? The Israelites. And they worship Him. Moses reaches God on the mountain, and the fire of God fills the mountain top. It's the same as the backside of the desert.

That, my friend, is where you'll worship.

Then, God said, ". . . *when* you have brought the people out of Egypt" (verse 12). He did not say *if* you bring the people out of Egypt. You see the difference, right? Because a wee bit later, Moses uses the words, "*if* I don't," but God never said *if* in this conversation. He said *when* and you *will*. As He always is, God was confident, consistent, and certain of what was going to take place.

Listen, God is our certainty.

Unchecked uncertainties breed deafness.

Moses isn't listening, is what I'm saying. Did you know when you're uncertain, you stop listening to what people are saying? Moses protested the second time. *If* I go, not *when* I go. He's already breeding uncertainty. Then that uncertainty grows. *If I go to the people of the of Israel and tell them the God of their ancestors had sent me to you, they will ask me, then what is His name? Then what should I say? What should I tell them?* Come on, man! You *do* know what to say. What you're doing, Moses, is trying to avoid your Next.

"I am who I am." Those are the holiest of terms associated with who God is. I am who I am. Say this to the people, "I am has sent me to you" (Exodus 3:14). Also, say this to the people: "Yahweh, the God of your ancestors, the God of Abraham, Isaac and Jacob" (verse 16) has sent me to you. And then He describes further by saying, "This is my eternal name, my name to remember through all generations" (verse 15). It was the most powerful name God would use. Jews never referred to that name in a public setting because it was so holy. But God used it to speak to Moses, requesting he use the name. That's a powerful thing for God to do.

When you're approaching your God-appointed Next, God says, "I'll put my name on it."

When God calls you to your Next, His name is on the line. If His name is on the line, let me tell you something . . . it's going to happen the way He wants it to happen.

As many people do, if I send people somewhere in my name, I typically remind them they are representing me. It's just a good nudge to preserve everyone's character and reputation. If God's willing to put His name on the line, do you think He is willing for it to be a failure or a success? Every time, the answer is a success. When God put His name on the line for Moses, it was a reminder of God's character, a wake-up call. "Can you hear me now, Moses?" he seemed to say. "I am the God that's sending you!"

Yet Moses protested again. When uncertainty is breeding more doubts, it's hard to be convinced. "What if they don't believe me or they say the Lord didn't appear to you? Then the Lord answered and said, 'What is that in your hand?' Moses said, 'a shepherd's staff.'" Shepherds lead.

If we don't believe what God is saying about us and what He is calling us to, then nobody else will believe it either. We have to believe! God is certain, and He is with us! And listen, God will give you everything you need even if it's a stick! He will equip you. To get to your Next, too many of us think we need to have the money, the network, the knowledge, and the resources. But that's a list we've dreamed up. God only needs us and maybe a stick! And we all know it isn't about the stick! It isn't about us!

Because if He put His name on it, whatever *it* is, it's all about Him.

When He calls you to your Next, He's about to show off through you.

Uncertainty can manifest in excuses. Sometimes, we even tell God how His plan cannot work because of our own weaknesses or sin. We do not see what He sees.

The call to our Next wakes up our uncertainty; uncertainty does not convince us, and then uncertainty questions if God is truly for us. Have you ever had one of those moments when you figure out what the Next is, and it makes you not believe?

- *Maybe it's not for me.*
- *Maybe it's for somebody else.*
- *Maybe I overheard God speaking to someone else.*

If Moses was trained in Pharaoh's household, he probably would have had something akin to a modern PhD-level degree. You're not raised in a king's house without getting an incredible education. Yet Moses uses the excuse that he can't speak well (i.e., eloquently). He can't speak well? Are you kidding me? This is not biblical, but I think the reason Moses said He's not good with words was that he had been on the backside of the mountain for so long that all he could hear was the sheep crying, *baaa, baaa, baaa.*

So Moses had started talking like the sheep: *I-I-I'mmm, I'mmm n-n-n-nota g-g-g-o-o-o-o-o-d w-w-w-with w-w-w-w-w-words, L-l-l-l-l-l-ord.*

If you have been speaking to sheep for forty years, how are you going to talk? I envision God speaking up, "Look, I've heard enough of what you're saying," and He asks Moses this very important question, "Who makes a person's mouth?" (Exodus 4:11). "Who decides whether or not people speak or do not speak? Hear or do not hear? See or do not see?"

Moses continues and says something like, "I don't have what it takes."

But God doesn't give up. He says to him, "I will be with you as you speak and I will instruct you in what to say" (Exodus 4:15). What He means is He is not only going to instruct Moses on when to speak, but He will tell him exactly what to say too.

If you're someone who believes they can't articulate messages well, God will help you. If you believe you don't know how to process thoughts, God will give you that skill too. Whether it's with words or something else, He will empower you.

God equips and empowers us for our Nexts, the ones He calls us to.

Your uncertainty will abdicate your Next.

Moses, essentially begs, "Please! Send anyone else" . . . I don't care who it is! Just not me Lord! And "the Lord became angry" (Exodus 4:13–14). Did you know God became angry with Moses?

Then God asked about his brother Aaron the Levite. Aaron spoke well. "And look! He is on his way to meet you now. He will be delighted to see you. Talk to him and put the words in his mouth. I will be with both of you as you speak, and I will instruct you both in what to do!" (Exodus 4:14–15).

Abdicate means to renounce or relinquish a throne, light, or power, or to claim responsibility, especially formally. Moses abdicated his Next when he asked God to send someone else. When you ask God about your Next and He calls you to what's next, don't look back and ask Him to call someone else. And don't second-guess Him or ask for something else to do.

Uncertainty gives rise to unbelief, which makes us doubt God. It makes you believe God's not enough. That His promises will be left unfulfilled.

I'm going to be with you.

I'm coming to rescue you.

You can use my name. I'm going to equip you.

Through your unbelief, you tell God, "It's not enough," just like Moses, who asked Him to send someone else.

Abdication says it's not about God; it's about me, and I just can't do it. You're going to stand before Jesus on Judgment Day, the one who hung on the cross. Don't be the one whose life said, "It's not about you." Because my guess is that Jesus is going to say, "What? Well, it wasn't about you! It was about me every time."

I think when we get to Heaven, we're going to see not only the things we've accomplished but also the things we never did but could have—were asked to do. I believe God will show us what could have been had we trusted His Next for our lives.

The good news in all this is that our uncertainty does not make God second guess—hallelujah! God's plan, our Next, is victorious (and always will be). When you ask God for what's next, and He gives you what's next, let me tell you what it comes with: it comes with a stick. It comes with His equipping power; it comes with His Words, which will work in you and through you, and it comes with His plan. He doesn't just call you, and that's it! He gives you a call with these things attached!

How can we ever have the audacity to say, "God, I appreciate your call—I really do—but I don't think your certainty is enough? I don't think your name is enough; I don't think your equipping me is enough, and I don't think your empowering me is enough. I don't think your plan is enough!"

Maybe the reason some believers are lacking substance or vitality is that we cannot believe what God says. We can't believe He's got our Next. The truth is, He's got your Next, your neighbor's Next, your friend's Next, your coworker's Next, your family's Next—everybody's Next, somebody's Next, and anybody's Next. He's got all of our Nexts.

So the big question: What's your Next? I don't know the answer, but I do know your Next comes with God's certainty! Your Next comes with God's name attached, a guarantee! Your Next comes with God's equipping power and empowering words! Your Next comes with His plans! and those are victorious plans!

When we're called to our Nexts, God expects an answer. He wants us to respond with, "Here I am." He expects us to do what Moses finally did in Exodus 4:18: "So Moses went." Those may be the most powerful words in this part of the story.

So Mike went.
So Johnathan went.
So Jeannie went.
So Jerry went.
So Mary went.

Just add your name and respond with steps of faith. Sometimes, God says we will start with a stick, much like Moses. Whatever we have, we should just go! Pick up our sticks and go.

We need to get out there and take our steps of faith. We won't know how it's going to turn out. We won't know what's going to happen. But we can go with certainty. Why? We're going with God's name. We're going with God's empowerment, and we are going with God's plan.

If you have any uncertainty about your Next, I want you to know that as I write these words, I am already praying with and for you and your Next.

PRAYER

Father, it's been a long time coming, but here we come! There's uncertainty with it, but God, you are our certainty. There is a certain uncomfortableness with it, but there's Your name attached to it. There's some amount of question, but there is equipping and empowering in You. There is some amount of wondering, yet I believe we will cease doubting if the glory of your plan is revealed through these encouraging and anointed Words. I pray they rest upon us.

We are listening for our Nexts, and when we get our calls to our Nexts, we will be certain of this: You, Lord, have our Nexts.

Let us know when the call to our Next is about to find us! For, we'll want to answer you, Lord. We know You will want an answer. So let us know when You are going to shake us up.

Then, when our Nexts are revealed, let us listen past our uncertainty to hear with clarity. Let us hear that it is You and Your name, oh Lord. We pray, Lord, that we will know we are Your people, with no doubts about it. We can do our Nexts. We have You so we have what it takes! God, I pray that You will download in us our Nexts, in the name of Jesus. Though we stumble, we will not fall because You will hold us. Your Word will illuminate our feet and light our paths as You expect us to walk in our Nexts, in Jesus's name. Amen. Thank you, Lord.

God's got your Next!

3

WHERE IS MY NEXT?

If location is everything, how do I find where my Next is?

G PS, God's placement system, gets us on the right path to our Nexts. This divine GPS is found in His Word. This is the starting place to find out *where* you are going. God spoke to my heart about that question above—Where is my next?—and He said this: *Mike, I have got your Next.*

FIRST, LET THERE BE LIGHT
Have you thought about what's next this week? Have you started to do something, forgotten what you were doing, and

wondered what was next? God has got every Next for you, even the ones you don't know or remember. In fact, the Scripture says, "The Lord directs the steps of the godly" (Psalm 37:23). Other translations say, *the steps of a good man—or righteous person—are ordered by the Lord.* The Lord delights in every detail of our lives. Every detail! Though we stumble, we will never fall, for the Lord holds us by the hand. The Lord is reaching to hold your hand today and every day.

Look at Psalm 119:105, "Your word is a lamp to guide my feet and a light for my path." This is important. If He has ordained every step and if He is directing every step, then we need to know what is illuminating our path. This Scripture tells us. Have you ever been lost in the dark without a flashlight? Have you prayed for light to be someplace, like right away? "God, You said You'd let there be light!" but no light came. Have you ever been scared in the dark? I'm going to assume that at one time or another, all of us have been lost or fearful in the dark. It's so easy to get disoriented when we can't see. There are no easily recognizable landmarks in the dark, just inky blackness. So when we are trying to find our way in life and it feels dark like that, we most want (dare I say, *need to have*?) to have our paths lit.

God's Word lights up our lives so He can direct every step. Why? He has got our Next.

SO WHERE IS NEXT?

I hope you have figured out that God has got your Next. You've learned He lights up your Next. Now, you may wonder *where*

Next is. You may be praying, "God, I get it. I trust You with my Next, but where is it?"

We would all love for God to show us our Next on demand, right? It rarely works that way. We all want the result, the victory, but we don't want to endure the journey to get there. Look, you don't have healing without sickness, and you can't have victory without the battles. There is a journey we all have to travel to get where we are going, to get to our Next.

Look at this part of the story in Moses's life, from Exodus 2–4: In Exodus 3:10, it says, "Now go, for I am sending you to Pharaoh. You must lead my people Israel out of Egypt." This is where Moses is called to his Next. God tells him to *go*. Then, in 4:20, the story continues, "So Moses took his wife and sons, put them on a donkey, and headed back to the land of Egypt. In his hand he carried the staff of God." Remember, Moses went. That was his response to God's call on his Next.

There's an entire part of the story that outlines the dialogue between these two, but I want to pull out some things in the story that might help us determine where our Next is located. Moses may have had a sense of his destiny, but he did not have a sense of his destination. In other words, he knew God had his Next, but he didn't know where his Next was going to take him. We may know God has something for us, but we don't know where it is. God knows your destiny and your destination *and* everything it will take to get there.

> When we dedicate ourselves to the Lord, we have to trust God
> with our destiny, destination, and the piece we often overlook,
> our development.

Let's go back to Exodus 2:13: "The next day, when Moses went out to visit his people again, he saw two Hebrew men fighting. 'Why are you beating up your friend?' Moses said to the one who had started the fight." Now, remember: what had happened the day before was that Moses had walked up to an Egyptian slave driver who had just beat down an Israelite. Moses was an Israelite raised in Egypt. Moses did not appreciate what he was seeing, and he had tried to negotiate the conflict into a better ending. But it got out of hand. Moses ended up murdering the Egyptian. In any culture, murder is murder . . . and murder is against the law, back then and today. If you read the entire Scripture in these chapters, you will find out Pharaoh was not happy. Pharaoh came after Moses because he killed the man. Suddenly, Moses is wanted for murder. All of this had happened in a twenty-four-hour period—before we read the account in Exodus 2:13 of the fight between the two Hebrew men.

Moses looked at the one in the wrong and asked him what he was doing. The guy responds something like this: "What are you going to do? Are you going to kill me like you killed the guy yesterday?"

Can we agree that this was a day of conflict management gone bad? Moses had a sense of his destiny, that he may be the deliverer of Israel, but he did not understand how to get to where he was going. He didn't even know where it truly was.

All he knew was that he was wanted for murder. He knew he had a destiny, though. He knew there was some destination, but he didn't know how to connect the dots. Did you ever play Connect the Dots when you were a kid? Did you lose? If you lose at Connect the Dots, it's usually because you cannot put the dots in the numbered order. Some kids might just go from one to one hundred and back to two, trying to get to the end as quickly as possible. But when they do, the complete picture never emerges. They reached the destination (one hundred), but they missed the journey that creates the beautiful image. Moses couldn't get from his destiny to his destination (one to one hundred); he could not connect the dots to see the beauty behind his God-ordained Next.

CHANGE YOUR PRAYER-SPECTIVE

There are Christ-followers today that are in such a position. They know they have a destiny; they understand God has got their Next, but they don't know where to put their quarter. Some Christ-followers don't know which game to play. They don't know where Next is located. Confusion sets in, and they don't know what to do. Well, this is your blessed day. If this describes you, I am going to help you find where your Next is!

First, I am not God (obviously). I will not speak to you as though I know your specific direction or location or even give you a possible road map. Here is what a lot of us do when we pray. We say, "God where is my Next?" Sometimes, we might even pray louder or with a more desperate tone, "O GOD, WHERE is my NEXT?" It doesn't work.

Let's redirect your prayer. Start praying: "God, will You light up my feet and light up my path with your Word?" With this prayer, you are going to get to your Next faster than you expected.

We often spend more time praying about the result than about the journey to the result. God wants you to *work* through the journey. He wants you to learn and grow on the way to your Next. This step-by-step journey prepares you to receive your Next, walk in your Next, and eventually lead from your Next. If God wanted to just get you there, it would be like *Star Trek*: a "beam me up, Scotty" kind of thing. No perseverance. No testing. No growth. If, as soon as you pray, God just moved you to where you needed to be, you'd be ill-equipped to handle your Next. Yet how many times have we prayed for God to do just that? To supernaturally translate us from one place to another? I have. God doesn't just want to get us there; He wants to take us on a spiritual journey. If God was more interested in getting us there than having us experience the learning and growing produced by the journey, then the moment we asked Jesus into our lives, he would just take us to Heaven.

Moses, in his sense of destiny, did not understand God's plan was to deliver the Israelites out of bondage in Egypt. Moses didn't see the whole picture. He had been raised in Pharaoh's castle. He had been raised to learn all the things he would need to learn. Moses was about forty years old when all in Exodus 2–4 happened, and he's just trying to find his way. He has the sense of purpose that he is supposed to help these people, but he doesn't know where that goes or how to get to where that goes. Let's look at what Moses learned in this journey, and then maybe we can learn from him.

THE JOURNEY IN EGYPT

Moses was willing to negotiate a stay in Egypt. He tried to negotiate conflict resolution with the slave driver and the Israelite slave. The Israelites wanted to be rescued from their Egyptian slave drivers, not continue to be residents in slavery.

Moses, after he has had this conversation with this Hebrew guy in Exodus 2:13, gets scared. He thinks everyone must know what has happened, what he did. Wanted for murder, he flees into the desert. When he gets out into the desert, some of his future father-in-law's family and workers find him. The first thing they report about him after he has helped them with their flock is that he is an Egyptian.

They tell everyone Moses is an Egyptian who has rescued them. Do you get the significance of this? Moses is not an Egyptian; he is a Hebrew. He must have still looked Egyptian, his upbringing and the culture had not fallen off of him yet. Don't miss the meaning.

There is a consequence when trying to follow our destinies but still holding on to our old lives. A lot of us are trying to find our destinations, but we are not willing to release our old journeys. We will go on a journey with God as long as we can drive the car. Once the road gets bumpy and Jesus requests the wheel, we kick him out of the car.

Moses had tried to negotiate a stay in Egypt when God was instead preparing him to negotiate the release of the captives.

God had no intention of keeping the Israelites in Egypt. He never did. When he sent them under Egyptian rule, He did not tell them to stay here forever. They were to stay for a season.

God wants us all out of Egypt, and here is why: Egypt in the Bible is a symbol of sin. It is a reflection of missing the mark or God's plan for us. So when God puts you in a situation and you sin or you miss the mark, God will never negotiate so that you stay where you are in the sin. He has (and always will) called you out. He didn't come in the flesh as the Son of Man to die on the cross so that you would stay in Egypt. He came to die on the cross for you to find and live in freedom.

When Moses ran into the desert, he still looked like Egypt, smelled like Egypt, and acted Egyptian, so everyone thought for sure that he was an Egyptian. We don't read, "Here is a Hebrew." Moses was still attached to his old life, even after he left it and negotiated his own way. Even tried to set up his own path and force the next step. When you take your own next steps, you will never get to the Next that God has for you. When you try to negotiate the part of God's plan that seems to be missing when you say, "I can hold on to God *and* live the way I want to live," then, the way you want to live is probably not how God said for you to live. It's not the destination God designed you to reach—nor the journey he calls you to live.

OUR RIGHTEOUSNESS

God said there is none who is righteous—not one—except Christ. Christ became our righteousness. We have no righteousness of our own accord. We have no right standing. We are not able to accomplish our destiny on our own. And we certainly can't do it with our own mindset, our own hands, or our own hearts. If we could, the law would have been good enough. The law was taken away when Jesus came and brought with him a new covenant, filled with grace. Grace says: *Trust Me with your Next and walk in the steps that I direct for you to get there.*

You can't drive your car of life. Have you ever seen that bumper sticker that says *Jesus is my co-pilot*? I don't believe that's a good thing. I believe Jesus better be the *pilot*. There was a time when I tried to drive my life. I drove it right off the edge of a cliff. I even reached the point where I tried to end my own life. There's no way I can drive my own life.

Early on, no one ever told me about my destination options. My destination is the same destination as your destination if Jesus is driving our lives. If you don't understand that, well . . . maybe I can help you. The Bible talks about Heaven and Hell. Heaven is the place Jesus is driving us to. Hell is the place we drive ourselves to, with the help of our enemy. Don't ever say Jesus sends us to Hell. That is the furthest thing from the truth. Jesus has given us destination options, but he drives us to Heaven.

When we want to be in control, we drive our lives away from God. When Jesus is driving our lives, we won't have to guess if we are going to make it to Heaven or not. If Jesus is the pilot, he has only got one destination. He has only got clearance on one runway. Everyone who has responded to his love, everyone who has become a Christ-follower, is headed to

Heaven forever, for an eternity with God. Tell somebody today about your final destination. You may get to help them make their reservation on the same trip itinerary.

Moses needed his encounter with the burning bush of God to understand his destiny and Israel's destination. For Moses, this experience with the supernatural God would lead him to his destiny. God told Moses, you will not do this by yourself. I got you. Moses may have missed this promise in the calling. Therefore, he went through all the stuff you went through. He missed it. He missed his destiny. He was not supposed to be the deliverer; he was supposed to be the facilitator. God is always the deliverer. The encounter at the bush would define the destination because in the same call—same verse—not only can you find the destiny, *I have come down to rescue them.* God also defined the destination: *to bring them out of that land.* In other words, we ain't negotiating with Egypt; we are not supposed to negotiate with sin. We are not going to stay in our lost places, our desert lands, or our captivity; we will not be enslaved anymore.

THE CALL CONTINUES

This one encounter with the God of the burning bush not only changes the destination of an entire nation, but it also shaped the next forty years of Moses's life. All the incredible life you read about Moses after this, until he dies, can be traced back to the burning bush. When you have an encounter with the King, as Moses had, it will reveal not only the one true destiny but also your destination. One encounter with a holy God can shape many years of your life. I pray that today, before you finish reading, you have an encounter with God that shapes your life, that you'll meet God—even within these pages—and He will reveal your Next. God has our Nexts; God has our destinies. Our destination is where the Next is located. If you are still looking for both your destiny and your destination, then look for an encounter with God.

His Word is a lamp and light to our feet and our paths. We need an encounter with the Word. The word became flesh, and it made his dwelling among us.

Who is the Word? That Word is Jesus, the King of kings, the Lord of lords, the soon-coming King of the world. That is the Word that we need an encounter with. We don't need Him just in the moment of salvation; we need Him every day, every month, every year. We need an encounter with God that will direct our destinies and define our destination.

Just take a moment—right now—and confess this to Him: *I am going to have an encounter with the Word that will reveal my destiny and my destination. Our destiny gets us to our destination.*

Our Next brings us to our crossroads. We will have choices to make and directions to choose from. Our culture believes we can just all get along. Not in the Kingdom. The cross separates the righteous and the unrighteous. When we face Jesus and the cross, there is a righteous way to live and an unrighteous way to live. There's a righteous relationship to be had and an unrighteous relationship. Yes, Jesus is the Prince of Peace, but he also told us he did not come to bring peace. He said that children would be against parents, and brothers and sisters would be against one another. When you make the choice to serve Jesus, it shifts your life, your destination. Your destiny is rewritten. Your Next reveals something you never understood before. There is a choice to be made: Will you follow your destiny to get to the destination that God has established, or are you are going to keep driving your own car?

Knowing your destination begins with knowing what it isn't. It isn't Egypt. It isn't missing His plan.

It is easy to buy into the lie that comes straight from Hell, from the devil himself, the father of lies, who tries to speak into your life: *You can't help who you are. You will just keep living like you are living. Change is not possible.*

Those, my friend, are lies. The devil believes all of that because he is a fallen angel, incapable of redemption. But Jesus didn't die on the cross for you to keep living in a lie. Jesus died on the cross for you to be set free.

On your journey, you may trip, but the Bible says you won't fall if you are holding His hand. I was recently walking with my granddaughter and she tripped. I grabbed her so she didn't fall. That reminded me of how God holds my hand. If I take Him by the hand and I trip along the way, he's going to catch me, pull me up, and keep me walking in the right direction.

THE DIRECTIONALS

Longitude and latitude is a system of numbers that tells you where you are. There are specific longitudinal and latitudinal values for where I am seated right now, as I write these words, and where you are right now while reading them. We now have phones and GPS devices that give us directions to get to very specific locations, or longitudes and latitudes. In a world where so many are directionally challenged, we are thankful for these directional devices and the system of longitude and latitude.

My dad was a stickler about quality directions. Here is what he said: "Don't say, 'Go down by that oak tree and turn left by the pine tree, and then go down the road to find the stump and turn left' because somebody might cut all that down before you get back. So you need to know where North, East, South, and West are." It's sage advice. When you are out in the world, whether walking around mega cities across the world or driving in the countryside, North is always North, South is always South, East will forever be East, and West is one hundred percent West. Whether I am at the southernmost tip of Africa or the southernmost point in the United States, it doesn't matter; whether I'm on an island in the Mediterranean or one in the Caribbean; whether I'm in Europe, Russia, or the outback of the Yukon Delta in Alaska where you must take a plane or a boat to get where you're going, North is North, South is South, East is East, and West is West.

What I'm saying is that much like a compass, God has a global positioning system too, and His global positioning system is available to all of us. It can help us find our destinies and destinations, our Nexts. That system is the Word, which is a lamp unto my feet and light unto my path. The Word directs our every step. If we are going to find where our Next is, we cannot keep walking around in the dark. We must light up our life with His illuminator, the Word. Our destiny and destination might just be good, spacious land, a land filled with milk and honey.

SUMMARY

Our Next begins with an encounter with Him. For Moses, the encounter happened in the sand at the borders of a burning bush. I don't have any bushes to burn. I am not God. But you need to seek an encounter with Him. In that encounter, you will find your destiny and your destination. Our Nexts are in our destiny. And in our Nexts, we will find the coordinates for our destinations.

If we don't have an encounter, we don't get the directions for taking the next step. We want a blessed life. To find it, we want to step in the right direction. The next step will get you there. Be sure to keep stepping, even when you don't like some of the steps you must take.

Where is your Next? It lives within a destined journey. That is why I encourage you to spend many times, periods of days, each year fasting and praying. Prepare yourself and be on the lookout for encounters with God. I am praying for you, that your season of fasting and prayer set up the next forty years of your life. That you encounter God and discover your Next . . . and that it will define for you your God-ordained destiny and earthly and eternal destinations.

4

ARE WE THERE YET?

Discovering the timeline to our Nexts.

I was immersed in the Ocala forest for three days, praying. Praying for my family, praying for our church, praying for the city I served. For years, I hid myself away every so often to pray in a cabin in the forest just to get away. To be in a place where I am disconnected from everything but God.

This particular year, I was more disconnected than ever. There had been a couple of occasions when, as I took prayer walks through the forest, if I stood beside a particular pine tree and lifted my left leg, I could get a signal on my cell phone. I went to that pine tree for three straight days but never got a signal. I went to the secondary place I had discovered, where I had to climb through some swampy terrain to get to it, but I could not get a signal there either. I took those circumstances as indicators from the Lord because every other year, I could get at least one bar of cell service in those spots. I had traditionally used that service to text my family and say, "I'm okay. I haven't been eaten by a bear yet." This time, I wouldn't have any outside communication until the last morning, when I was getting ready to come back from my prayer retreat.

On that last morning, I went to my primary spot, and my phone displayed "LTE" service, which is better than G3—if you know what I mean. With the LTE, I can do anything I want: call, text, or even video call. I think it was the Lord saying, "I want you to myself for three days." And He had gotten all of me. It was just Him and me . . . well, and the other animals—like the bears.

For those three days in the wilderness, though, I knew God was with me. I knew God was speaking to me, and I felt compelled to continue praying and fasting. I'd pray and drink and read and drink and pray again, diving into God's Word in the forest. Here's what happened:

The Lord directs the steps of the godly; he delights in every detail. [Every detail.] *Though they stumble, they will never fall, because the Lord holds them by the hand* (Psalm 37:23).

We should pray, "Lord, hold me by the hand."

God directed me to a particular book, to a particular passage, and it just broke me. In the first chapter, I read a statement that was so good. It fit my heart. But there was nothing really amazing about it. More like a sense that the statement was good. At the end of the chapter, in the last paragraph, the author went back and related the latter content to that first statement, that one sentence that had grabbed me and not let go. And I just lost it in the cabin, weeping before the Lord. I even remember what I said: "I didn't see that coming." *I didn't see that coming.*

Sometimes, that's how God works. He just wants you to Himself. He just wants you in solitude. He just wants you quiet. He just wants and only you. So here is how God challenged me on this prayer retreat. The statement was about sacrifice. *Bring the first-fruit offering.* Not just our regular tithe. We must come with something extra to seal the deal on this fast. We must go to God with our offerings, saying, "God, I have given you my time. I have given you my food (or whatever we may have fasted), but I want to give you all of my resources too. I believe You're going to take care of my whole year." Maybe it is a "Seed Faith" offering. But while reading that book, I knew I had to pray that week and then give my "first-fruit offering," the first, best fruit of the year offering, just to say, *I love you, Lord.*

My offering would be a testament to God as it communicated, "Lord, You have the next year of my life, so I want to plant something financially in Jesus for this next year."

Each step of our Nexts will come, even if unexpectedly, if we will listen to and obey every directive He gives.

STRETCHING INTO OUR NEXTS

God has a way of calling us to things that stretch our faith and grow us. The things He challenges us with are so big we cannot do them without Him. If we can accomplish things without Him, we wouldn't need Him. If He stretches us, and we trust Him through the discomfort, we can watch Him do amazing things through and for us.

I have seen God give people jobs; I have known people who were out of work for nine months, then get an offer for a job that pays three times more than their last job because they were faithful, even while out of work. Let the Word of God be a lamp to your feet and your path, guiding you all the way. God's got your Next. Sometimes, it just takes steps of faith out of our comfort zones.

Every time I spend a season fasting and in prayer, God answers those prayers. Sometimes, it happens days, weeks, months, and even years later. But it's amazing when He does that.

Moses also heard from the Lord in prayer, but God did not do everything He set out to do right then. We often ask, "When is it coming?" when our patience wears thin. Have you ever been traveling on a long road trip when your kids or others in the car get bored, tired, or are just plain ready to arrive? What are they saying? *Are we there yet?*

When you were a kid, I bet you asked your parents the same thing. I remember asking that of my dad, and my dad was not too receptive to that question, especially when we traveled. It was not wise to utter it more than once in his car; otherwise, the trip would be a done deal, right then and there. Sometimes, he just gave me *the look* and if I got the look, then I knew: Don't ask anymore.

Don't ask no more was the environment I grew up in. It's okay. I didn't have to attend any counseling for that. But this is now what I do with my kids every time they ask, "Are we there yet?"

I say, "Five more minutes." Five more minutes, no matter how long it is. When we didn't arrive at our destination in five minutes, they asked again. "Are we there yet?"

"Five more minutes."

Then, as they got older and a little sassier, I decided to be a little sassier with them too. "Are we there yet?"

"Does it look like it!?!?"

Okay. I didn't say that. But I wanted to; you know every parent does!

How does it make you feel as a parent when your kids keep asking you, "Are we there yet?" Annoyed? Irritated? Aggravated or frustrated, right? We all feel that way. How do you think God feels when we keep asking Him, "Are we there yet?" He's our heavenly Father. We are on a trip with Him, a journey. How are we looking at that journey? Is the question, *Are we there yet,* flowing from our mouths every time we pray? Some days, I wonder if God might love to send us to the answering machine or stop our road trips and turn around.

WE'RE NOT ALONE

Before we throw stones at one another, David, the great king, the great leader, did the same thing. Go read the Psalms. How many times did David ask, "How long, oh Lord?" Psalm after Psalm after Psalm, David, while running for his life, while leading, and even while things are not going well or remotely close to the way he thinks they ought to happen, asks the question. When he wasn't getting to his Next, he often included in his songs, "How long, O Lord . . . is this going to happen?"'

I would have loved to hear God's response. Just once. I'm glad that we don't; we might not appreciate it. I'm thankful that sometimes God doesn't speak to us in the moments of our folly or longing or childish questioning. If I was God—and I am not—and you asked me, "How long?" as many times as David did in the Psalms, I would probably say to you some things you don't wanna hear.

NEXT IS NOW

God relates to us through the things we know. We will find our Next when we understand the process of the Next. Eventually, we will understand our Next is really *now*.

It's true. You've got to let go of your now to get to your Next, but your Next is His now. So the implication here is that the now you are in is your plan. But God wants you to release that so that you can get into His now. Same time periods but different *dimensions*.

Do we always realize God is in a different dimension from us? He is with us, but we can't see Him. As humans, we are three-dimensional. You can even go look at how Paul prayed through that reality in his letter to the Ephesians. Paul had caught on to the dimensional aspect of our beings when he said, "I want you to know the love of Christ" as he writes in his second prayer to the Ephesians. Paul continued, ". . . And may you have the power to understand, as all God's people should, how wide, how long, how high, and how deep his love is" (Ephesians 3:18).

Paul added a fourth dimension to that prayer. Builders know we build in three dimensions. If we are building something, what are the three things we consider? Length, width, and height. If you go back and read that letter, you'll notice Paul had discerned that God resides in a different dimension. His love is in a different dimension. His love spread four dimensions: width, depth, length, and height.

To get to where God is, we have to find His dimension. We have to move in faith. That means it's not our now, it's His now. *Next is now.*

As we step to our Next, God will give us what we need. We often first want what we think we need before we take our step to our Next. More money. More courage. More skill. More faith. God doesn't work that way. Even in their journey, when the Israelites got to the Red Sea carrying the Ark, they had to put their feet in the water before it would separate. Noah had to close his Ark and seal it for seven days before the rain came.

If you study story after story after story throughout the Scriptures, you'll find few prerequisites for the people of God to take their steps before God will do what He says He will do.

He wants us to see that we have to trust Him, that we have to take a step of faith in everything we do. Just like Moses, who went. And when we walk in faith, God speaks.

From the bush, God spoke His directive words; He laid the path for Moses. After Moses went back to Jethro, after he went back to his family, and after he started on his way, God spoke to him. After Moses had been out in the desert for forty years, God spoke to him and told him to return. And when Moses went to Midian, God spoke: "Now the Lord had said to Moses in Midian, go back to Egypt for all those who wanted to kill you are dead" (Exodus 4:19). Wouldn't it have been good to have that information beforehand? I mean, maybe Moses wouldn't have argued with God six times if he already had that information.

God will give us information on a need-to-know basis. Military people use the phrase "need-to-know." In other words, your commander is going to give you information that will help you succeed on your mission, but you will not get it until you need to know it. God, our commander-in-chief, sends us out and when he does, he will give us information on a need-to-know basis. After Moses starts toward Midian, still in the desert, making steps towards obeying God, then God says to him, oh, by the way, Pharaoh, the one who wanted to kill you is dead. There is a new King in town and they will not kill you anymore. Moses might have been thinking, *Could You have said that earlier?* It's a faith-builder—a circumstance in which we must move in obedience to our Next without having all the information we think we need. If I were Moses, I'd probably still be dreading this course of action on the inside. As he's likely dreading things, God says, by the way, the guy who wants to kill you is not there anymore, so you will be all right . . . oh, and he has been gone for forty years! What!?

God speaks to him again. Check this out, and see: As we take our next step, God will give us what we need and what we need to know. Look at verse 21: "So, Moses put his wife and sons and put them on a donkey and head them back to the land of Egypt. In his hand, he carries the staff of God, (we talked about the staff) and the Lord told Moses, when you arrive back in Egypt, go to Pharaoh and perform all the miracles that I have empowered you to do."

An interesting note here: There were three miracles God said He'd provide for the Israelites for them to even believe Moses. Yet it was ten plagues for Pharaoh. God encourages Moses to do the miracles He had empowered him to do. Listen, this won't make sense, God says, but I will harden his heart, Pharaoh's heart, *making it stubborn,* so Pharaoh will refuse to let the people go (Exodus 7:3). God told Moses, *I am sending you not to a hard task, but to an impossible task. And it's my fault.*

How many people believe that God just makes it all easy? He doesn't. It's never all easy with God. Why? Because he's building—and I put a question mark by *faith-builder* here— but it really is a faith-building moment. God didn't tell Moses the guy that wants to kill him is no longer there and that he was no longer wanted for murder anymore until *after* Moses has taken the step toward Midian. Only, once Moses loads up his family and moves, taking the next steps toward Egypt, God speaks to him again and says, *Oh, guess what I forgot to mention to you about Pharaoh. I'm going to harden his heart, and he's not going to hear anything you have to say.*

When Moses had argued about this path, he never asked, "What about Pharaoh?" Moses wanted to know about the Israelites. He asked God, "What if they don't believe me?" He never asked if Pharaoh would believe. Or how. Yet God says, I'm going to harden his heart so that he refuses to let my people go. Then you will tell him, this is what the Lord says, "Israel is my firstborn son; I command you to let my son go so that he would worship me, but since you have refused, I will now kill your firstborn son" (Exodus 4:22–23, my paraphrase).

It was heavy when Moses thought the Israelites were going to have him for lunch; now it's more serious when he realizes Pharoah is going to make him for lunch too. This is unbelievable—that God would call him to such a task. Sometimes, we can lose sight of God's requests for us. We might think to ourselves, *That was Moses. God will never call* me *to such a task.* Maybe he would not call you to a such a task; but if a task seems impossible, you can only do it with Him. And that's what God is after. The impossibilities. The faith-building Next. Maybe that's the faith-building Next Moses needed.

God doesn't share with Moses anything about Pharaoh being dead or that there's a new Pharaoh in town. When we step out to our Nexts, God will give us what we need and what we need to know at the need-to-know time. It's not always what we want to hear or do. Let me ask you something. Can God still be God to us if we don't get the answers we want?

Don't answer too quickly. Because for most of us, when we don't get the answer we want, we are like that kid that says, "Are we there yet?" We doubt, we pout, we cry, and we run.

I DIDN'T SEE THAT COMING

One Sunday evening, during the "alter time" at church, I lay face-down on the stage, throwing a fit, beating my fists, and kicking my feet in insubordinate prayer. Later, I'd discover my toes were black and blue with bruises from my tantrum. The night became a life-changing encounter for me.

I was preparing to travel on another mission trip. Over ten years, I had led nearly thirty such trips while my kids were coming up through elementary school. At this point, my children had reached middle and high school, and I didn't want to go on mission trips anymore. I didn't want to leave my kids. Worried questions filled my mind.

- *What if I don't come back to them?*
- *What if something tragic happens while I'm gone?*

Those questions flooded my mind, and I wanted to give up going on mission. In reality, I was fighting against doing what God told me to do. I had to learn to release my kids to the Lord. I had dedicated each of them when they were babies—a promise I now wanted to renege on. Hence my tantrum. I realized I had to release them all over again that Sunday night. But I just didn't want to surrender.

I don't know how long it took for me to throw my tantrum. It seemed like an eternity, but I'm sure it was only thirty minutes or an hour, at most. Almost everyone had left by the time I finally got up with my bruised fists and feet. I'm not normally prone to temper tantrums, but I sure threw one that night with my Father. Once I stood up, I looked down the aisle to find one of my leaders—actually the missions director. And that missions director, Jim, said to me, "Pastor, are you okay?"

"Jim, I need to ask you something."

"What is it, Mike?"

With tears running down my cheeks and a lump in my throat, I said, "I just need to ask one question."

"What's that?"

"If I die while I'm a pastor of this church, and especially if I'm on a mission trip, I need you to promise me one thing. Make sure you take care of my kids. Make sure that my wife and kids don't go hungry, that they find a place to live . . . they find a way to make it in life. I just need somebody to help me, to step in so they will all be all right."

Jim looked at me, now with tears in his eyes, and replied, "Pastor, I will do that but under one condition."

"What?"

Jim said, "You will do the same for my kids and my family."

I smiled for the first time all evening. "You got it, Jim."

Here's the craziest part of this story. Jim had become my missions director after a successful career at the Department of Transportation. At fifty-one years old, he received his credentials. He was preparing to become a full-fledged missionary, readying to go into the mission field. Do you know what happened next? At age fifty-two, Jim died after a heart attack. As I had promised, I helped to take care of his kids and his wife, who was also my personal assistant at our church office. Neither of us had any idea what that moment at that altar service late that Sunday evening would soon lead to. But God knew. Our lives were forever altered that night.

You don't know where the action is always going to be, but you know it's coming. It's coming in your Next step. It's coming in your now; it's coming in your now because it's His now. Let Him speak to you.

During that alter time, I did not want to hear God say, "You've got to go, anyway." I thought He would love me and be compassionate and say, "Michael, I understand. You don't have to go." He didn't say that. Do you know what he said? "Buckle up soldier, let's go! You're telling Me, after I released my Son and He died on the cross, that you want to whine? Let's go!"

So I said, "Okay." Well, not exactly. After about an hour of my childish tantrum, I said, "I got it. Yes, sir."

UNEXPECTED HELPERS IN YOUR NEXT

The next thing that happened to Moses in Exodus is unbelievable. After God said He would harden Pharoah's heart, God sent a couple of unexpected people to stand with Moses.

I never thought it would be Jim for me.

I first went to that church to serve as a youth pastor. I served for five years, and Jim's daughter and son were in the youth group. His daughter was a high school junior when I arrived. I told the youth group we were taking a mission trip that summer. Well, we took a big team, maybe fifteen students on that first mission trip, and Jim's daughter, Jennifer, was one of the students. Jennifer had said to me, "I want to go, but my dad won't let me." I prayed with her and advised her to keep praying. She went home and told her dad about the trip and all the details.

Jim said, "No, no, no, no. You're not going." Finally— because you know how daughters can be . . . they can bat their eyes and cry and Daddy's will change their minds—"Oh, we'll figure out something."

Dads know what I'm talking about. We call that being "wrapped around the little finger" syndrome. Well, Jim finally relented, and here is how did it: He said, "I will let you go if you can raise every dollar for the trip (about $1,300). You cannot take it out of your savings, and I will not give you a dime."

In two weeks, Jennifer had all of the money. Two weeks. She was the first one who paid in full, and Jim had to eat his words. The end of the story was that Jim became my missions director, traveling on multiple trips. His wife, who also took multiple mission trips, became my personal assistant when I became the lead pastor. And later, Jim's son would become the missions director of his church and go on multiple mission trips. A family legacy built on mission. And it had all started with a father who relented and learned to support missions through giving, who would eventually submit again and go on mission trips himself.

Let me tell you what God will do in your life. He will send unexpected people to help you. Jim was an unexpected person who God sent into my life, one who helped me through my "altering process."

Don't give God the opportunity to move on from you. Don't let Him give your Next to someone else. Ask the Israelites; ask leaders throughout the Scriptures. God moved on from many of them. The Pharisees, the Jewish ruling counsels, were all people who God moved beyond because they would not respond to His way. Ask the seventy-two elders that led the Israelites up to the edge of the Promised Land but would not believe what Caleb and Joshua had to say. Ask the ten spies if God won't move on from you. They all know the pain of missing their Nexts. God will move on beyond you if you don't trust Him. You just understand—you must know in the deepest parts of your heart and soul—that God's got you. He's got your Next, and He's got every step along the way. Look for the people He will put in your path to help you. You'll see them.

5

NEXT IS NEXT

Our Next is one in a series of Nexts.

My fifth Next in ministry landed me in the place I believed I would grow old. I said I was going to be a seventy-five-year-old youth pastor who worked with students. It was a blessed season for me. Many students came to be followers of Christ. Many leaders answered God's call to ministry. God gave us favor in many ways.

However, much to my amazement, God had another Next for me five years later, one that changed the destiny of my entire ministry. He moved me from youth ministry to adult ministry as a lead pastor in the same church. Let's just say I did not see that coming. The blessing and favor continued and increased. Again, many came to the Lord and our outreach grew to reach literally around the world.

I then assumed I would retire in that role, in that church. However, after ten years as the lead pastor, God revealed another Next. This time, it was one that would expand my ministry in new and amazing ways. Each of these Nexts developed me for the place He was taking me next. Each Next helped to prepare me for the Next I am in today!

Sometimes, we think our Next is the end of the journey.

Next is usually not the end; next is simply next.

Here is what most of us want: We want our Nexts to be the end. We don't want to go through anything else because—let's face it—Nexts are often the hard parts of our journeys.

As we should do, let's get back to the Bible. In Moses's story, he thought his Next was to relocate the entire nation—physically—from Egypt to the Promised Land, all in one move. *All in one move.* Some of us want our Nexts to be places where nothing else goes wrong, where nothing else negative happens.

If that were true, then the moment we accept Jesus into our lives and become Christ-followers, we would die and go to Heaven. Let me ask you: Are you already a Christ-follower? Are you living obediently to His Word, and is He your Lord?

Now, I'm not sure about this, because I'm not able to see you right now—and I am no medical doctor—but you are still living and breathing since you are reading this book. And if you're also a Christ-follower, it means your Next was not the end. Because if becoming a saved soul is a Next (and it is!), and the Next is the end, God would have immediately taken you to Heaven and your earthly life would have been over for you. Instead, He designed our lives to be filled with Nexts, Nexts that compile into a journey. It's a journey with the ultimate goal of getting to Heaven.

Unfortunately, our cultural Christianity (in the United States) often intimates that it's more valuable to be blessed in this lifetime than to make it to the next lifetime. God is not just interested in you being blessed. Yes, He will bless you, but His goal is to get you to eternity with Him. That is what will glorify Him. So if you are reading this book to discover how to be more blessed in this life, let me tell you, you are missing the greatest opportunity of your lifetime. The greatest opportunity of this lifetime is to prepare yourself for the next lifetime.

I want to help you get there, to make sure nothing takes you away from that eternal appointment. I love you. I don't want to spend eternity without you. (I'm just saying this as kindly yet truthfully as I know how to say it.) I'm not living to spend this lifetime with you. I'm living to get us both to Heaven to spend eternity with God. I believe Heaven is real; I don't believe it's just a made-up storybook destination to fit a storybook journey. I believe it is exactly why God sent Jesus to redeem humanity—not so we can be blessed in this lifetime, but to pave the way for getting you to your Nexts (plural). Because remember, Next is not the end; Next is simply next.

Moses learned quickly that his Next was *not* the Promised Land, as he assumed. He is supposed to be going there, and he ended up going to *the edge of* the Promised Land. But Moses did not get to live there. He set his feet in the Promised Land, but that didn't happen in the Old Testament. It was in the *New Testament* where Moses meets with Jesus on the mountaintop, and at that moment, they were in the Promised Land.

In Exodus, Moses's Next was not the Promised Land. His Next comprised *the steps* to the Promised Land. Taking the steps to get to your destination but not actually getting there are not the directions you want to hear. Talk about an inconvenient journey, maybe even a demotivating one!

Moses's first few steps on this Next journey brought him to his father-in-law, who he had been with for forty years. Moses said, "Hey, I appreciate everything that we have together and the business we have built, but the truth is, I'm going to take my wife (your daughter) and my kids (your grandkids) and move back to Egypt where I'm wanted for murder. Oh, and we are going to deliver the entire Israelite community that didn't want me around to help them when I left." I put quotes here, but this is just me filling in the story from my imagination of how it must have gone down. How do you tell your father-in-law something like that? I know many people who don't have good relationships with their in-laws. Imagine having to tell them something like this? What are they going to say? Well, Jethro, Moses's father-in-law—evidently a man of God—said, "Okay, see you later." That's pretty cool, but I mean just think of the moment, *the moment* of having to tell your father-in-law all of that and then having him agree and offer this kind of support! Wow! Just, wow!

Then Moses had to speak with Aaron—his brother, the co-heir to a slave's inheritance. And Aaron is on his way. Some scholars believe these two may have had some kind of relationship, but by most accounts, it appears it was a distant one, at best. Moses is going to meet with Aaron and try to convince Aaron that though it didn't work out before in Egypt, God wants Moses to try again.

I imagine that your brother, like many others in your immediate family, might usually be the first to second-guess you. Your family might think, say, or simply can't hide the expressions on their faces that say, "Really?" (insert sarcastic tone). Understand, they have seen you make mistakes; they have seen you fail; they have seen you not accomplish things you've set out to do, and they have seen you not finish what you started.

Aaron was told by God to go meet Moses in the wilderness. They met at the mountain of God. Aaron greeted his brother Moses with a kiss. This was a sign of acceptance and love between brothers. When God is sending you to your Next, He will prepare the way for you, including making a way for you and your family.

After Aaron, Moses then has to meet with the seventy-plus elders. Have you ever met with seventy elders of a church? Well, with any number of elders, those meetings are difficult. Moses had to convince them he was supposed to deliver a million Jews out of slavery, into a promised land, which they knew nothing about. And somehow, by the grace and power of God, Moses does it.

Then, he has to meet with Pharaoh. Times ten. Moses goes to Pharaoh; then he goes back to Pharaoh. Again and again. Each time, one of the plagues or miracles is unleashed. Ten times! Unbelievable, right? And remember, Pharoah is the guy whose heart God has hardened. Yet Moses has to keep going back to him. This can't be easy.

How would you feel? How would you process all of this? How would you respond? If God said, "I'm going to harden the heart of the whole church (or ministry) you are leading, but you are going to convince them to do something. Ten times, I will go to them, and every time, that ministry, those leaders' hearts, will get even harder."

Pharoah responded. He drove the Israelites further into slavery. He did all kinds of nasty stuff—until God unleashed the tenth plague, the one where Pharoah lost his son. Finally, Pharoah said, "Go, get out!" I don't know if I would have persevered as Moses did. I just don't know about trip numbers seven, eight, or nine. I may have given up. Maybe you are more spiritual than I am.

I have been a member of a state board, which requires me, among other things, to sit in a boardroom at least four times a year. As I sit in all of these boardrooms, the things we are hoping and working for seem to take forever to move forward or change. It's difficult to keep going back when there is no momentum or change. In fact, it feels like we're moving backward or as if things are getting worse. Have you ever heard the adage, *It gets worse before it gets better?*

Between some of those trips that Moses took to meet with Pharoah, he goes back to talk to the elders. He also had to go talk to the Israelites still in slavery, and you know what they wanted to do? Kill him. I'm going to express it here in Southern terms . . . *They wanted to kill him dead.* I don't know how you kill any other way, but they surely want to kill him dead. Moses has to convince this group that wants him dead that they are still supposed to wait patiently to be free. Over and over, Moses had to keep going back to offer encouragement because they were the ones who would get mistreated every time he went to Pharaoh and God unleashed a plague.

Once Pharoah finally let the Israelites go, Moses and the freed Israelites come to an expansive and impassable sea. With a million fellow Jews in tow, Moses faces Pharaoh again. This time it is an angry Pharaoh, who is coming after him . . . to kill him dead. The Israelites around him aren't done with him yet, either. They are ready to kill him, too, as they stand in that valley, anticipating being slaughtered by Pharoah and his army. Go read the story, it's amazing.

This is why Moses is called one of the greatest leaders of all times. The Bible calls him that. I don't know anybody that could have—that would have—managed this scenario the way Moses did. Maybe his forty years in the backside of "Desert University" prepared him more than we'll ever realize.

Each step Moses took was a faith-builder step toward his Next. Of course, most of us know the story well enough to know God parted that sea and the Jews escaped as the waters closed around Pharaoh's men, who were still in hot pursuit. After Moses gets through the sea, he faces an enormous desert. The irony! (Or part of Moses's Next, which God had prepared him for in his earlier Nexts!)

Moving a million people on foot, with mamas with children and pregnant ladies, old folks, young folks, and all their goods through a desert, seems unfathomable. Maybe you have never been to a desert. I have been to two deserts. Let me tell you something; just moving your body through a desert for a short while is challenging. I've never been to Phoenix. Phoenix is a city that was built in the middle of the desert. When you go outside, you're literally in the desert, and there is no doubt about it. If you have ever been to Phoenix, *boom*! You've been in the land of sand and rock. There are no trees, no bushes, no nothing but brownness. I remember being in Phoenix a few years back, and as I walked from the hotel I was staying at to the convention center, it was 119 degrees outside. This is what the city-dwellers told me: "Oh, it's not the same as the heat you are used to! It is a dry heat." One hundred, nineteen—dry or wet—ain't fun. As soon as I walked out of the doors of the lobby, I was drenched, even though I wore light-weight clothes. It doesn't matter. Once it's 119, it's hot.

Imagine moving a million people, old and young alike—babies, farm animals, the whole deal—in 119-degree weather. It'd be a monumental task!

There was constant complaining. They didn't have enough to drink; they never had enough to eat, and they didn't have enough of the others things they needed. And Moses had to keep dealing with every complaint.

MORE NEXTS . . .

After the desert, they reach the mountain. This is the same mountain where Moses encountered the burning bush—Mount Horeb and Mount Sinai were the same mountain. Do you remember the sign God gave Moses? "The sign for you, the first place you're going to come back to is the same mountain and you're going to worship here." When they arrive, the Israelites begin to worship and Moses goes up the mountain to be with God. When he comes back down, there's a party going down, and that's when he noticed the golden calf. What happened? Well, Moses had the capacity to lead in a way that gave him an audience with God and an audience of golden-calf worshippers. I just don't know how Moses did it. Moses is an amazing leader.

God absolutely with take you through every step, but understand, Next is *next*, and every step you take is a faith-building step for the next Next.

> **Each Next prepares us for the next Next.**

Let's look biblically for the truth to this statement. First, David and the lion and the bear. With his bare hands, David had killed them (one Next). When he ultimately faced Goliath, I don't think he could have mustered the confidence if he hadn't killed the lion and the bear with his bare hands. I've killed some things with guns—I'm a hunter—but I have never killed anything with my bare hands. And I certainly haven't killed a lion or a bear with my bare hands. And, just in case you are curious, I haven't killed a giant with my bare hands. But David did. I bet those animals weren't his first fights, either. I think there were thieves he had to fight off; I think there were wild dogs or coyotes he had to handle; I think there were probably snakes and all kinds of natural elements that he had to fight off to protect his flock. He was a shepherd boy, so he had to fight . . . and fight and fight through life. By the time he stood with those stones and a sling in front of Goliath, he saw it as just another fight. The difference this time was David knew it was also God's fight. His Next arrived after a series of other Nexts, which prepared him for that day.

In our journey, each next prepares us for the next Next too.

GOOD NEXT VS. EVIL NEXTS

Look at this interesting verse in Luke: Jesus, during the end of one of his Nexts, when he endured his forty days of fasting—the only water kind of fast and forty days in the wilderness kind of fast—we know he wrestled with the devil. Look at what the Word says in Chapter 4, verse 13: "When the devil had finished tempting Jesus, he left him until the next opportunity came." You know what that means, right? That means the enemy was just setting up something else, his nefarious Next for Jesus, and he does the same with you.

Satan will try to get you off your Next for God. The enemy is setting up some Next for you to distract you from your good

Next, the one from and for God. *When the opportunity comes.* Do you know when the next opportunity comes? I think it comes when God is already setting you up for your God-ordained Next—when you are already stepping toward it. That's when then the enemy is going to get involved because if you are not stepping toward it, he wouldn't have anything to stop you from doing or being.

Look at Revelation 12:10. "For the accuser of our brothers and sisters has been thrown down to earth." In other words, the enemy is setting you up for your Next, and then he's going to the Father to rat you out and say, "[Your name] isn't getting it done." Satan will accuse you left and right, and he'll get others to do the same. They will accuse you at work, in the church, in the community, and maybe even in your family. When you are accused by people, yet you're innocent, listen to me: the enemy is somewhere in the middle of that deal.

When Satan is pushing his Nexts on you, you are stepping in the right direction. By the way, if you don't think the devil won't show up within the Church, look around the next time you are there; he might be there too. You can recognize him because he will be the one accusing believers of all kinds of things. Here is the good news: "No weapon turned against you will succeed" Isaiah 54:17). Weapons will be formed against you, but they will not prosper. The last words concerning the devil are that he will be hurled down. The enemy, even though he can gain access to God's presence, even though he will accuse you before God, is destroyed in the end.

LEARNING FROM EACH NEXT

I'm hammering this point home. Each Next prepares us for the next Next. We don't live in our pasts; we learn from them. It's the last test we had that will produce our testimony, which empowers us for our next Next.

Look at Revelations 12:11. "They [meaning believers] have defeated him [the devil because they are talking about the accuser of the brethren] by the blood of the Lamb (we can't do it on your own; pay attention to this next part) and by their testimony." A testimony doesn't come without a test, literally! The testimonies about how God helped us conquer our last Nexts empower us, giving us the strength we need to overcome and make it through the next Next. When I finally figured that part out—when I finally got that—I said, "Oh, God, thank you!"

When I'm going through something difficult, sometimes I say, "God, no!!" I am not always worried about what I'm going through; I am worried about what was coming next! If I was going through something *that* difficult, I knew at some point I'd make it through it and have a testimony. I just knew it was to going prepare me for more Nexts—bigger, more impactful Nexts. When you go through a tough time, it may be a small Next. If so, I can all but guarantee that the next Next will be a bigger one. Lion, to bear, to Goliath. Oh, my! Bear to Goliath, to caves, to king, to having a son that wants to kill you. That's David's path.

In the book of Revelation, it tells us the followers of Christ will overcome by the blood of the Lamb and the word of their testimonies, but *they did not love their lives, so much as to shrink back to death.* That's critical. You can't leave this part out. It's about a martyr's heart. Having a martyr's heart in any situation, I'm not backing down when it comes to obeying Jesus. What about you?

By the way, you don't have to go looking for death; it will find you. Some people get crazy in some religious circles and faiths—and even in some Christianity circles—and will die for their faith, like blowing themselves up. You don't have to go do that. You have to settle in your heart that when you face a moment of choice—obey God or not—you know what you will do. Decide *now* that you will not back down in doubt, but stand in your faith. You know why I'm telling you that? Because I want you to get to Heaven and have a resolve to get to Heaven.

So how do you learn? You take a step. You take one step. That's it. Each stepping stone inside each Next is a learning tool. A guide. It's filled with wisdom, and the experience of taking a step infuses you with knowledge and power. His power. Remember, the reason this book is called *Next: God's Got Your Next* is because as a teenager in the convenience store or arcade, when I wanted to play a video game but someone was already playing, I would put a quarter on the game and say, "I got next." God spoke to me and said, "Mike, I got your Next." I want you to know: God's got your next and every step between. He's your teacher. Every quarter has *In God We Trust* imprinted on it. Don't let a quarter out-trust you. The American Government, the American monetary system, will not help us to trust Him. They do, however, on each quarter, remind us to trust Him. I will trust God with my life. The challenge for all of his people, for the people who want to make it to Heaven, is that they have resolved in their hearts and minds, as followers of Christ, come Hell (literally) or high water, come the devil or his planned circumstances, they will not be stopped.

DON'T QUIT

I find it amazing how it's often the small things that make us mad. We want to quit God over quick trips, like the kid asking, "Are we there yet?" No, keep on trucking! Keep stepping! Put your quarter on the game. And keep playing. You have an opportunity ahead of you to make Heaven your home.

Next is not about getting to our pre-conceived ends in the fastest and easiest ways we know how. It is about getting to our *Now*, God's Next for us. Jesus said it like this: your mistake is that you don't know Scripture; you don't know the power of God.

Long after Abraham and Isaac and Jacob had all died, God said to Moses, "I am the God of your father—the God of Abraham, the God of Isaac, and the God of Jacob (Exodus 3:6, Matthew 22:32)," but He also says He is the God of the *living*, not the dead (Matthew 22:32). Right? These guys live! God is looking for somebody to take the steps that He has ordered. If you want to be dead, just go live in a funeral home. If you want to be alive, find a church that will encourage and support you in taking a step to where God wants you to go.

Step there. Don't quit. Step again. God said to Moses, "I AM WHO I AM. Say this to the people of Israel: I AM has sent me to you."

God didn't say *I was* had sent him. God used the present tense. God is the god of the present. He's the God of *right now*. He is the God of your right now. He is the God of your Next, your now, your steps.

DON'T LIVE IN THE PAST

Sometimes, we live in our pasts. We may have had some glory in our histories—times when God did something that was really wonderful, and we are still living there in our minds. Shake yourself and get free. Yes, maybe it was good. Really good. Or maybe it was bad. Maybe we have been running from God. Maybe we have been hurt. (I've been hurt a lot, I'd argue as much as the next guy). We've all been beaten down, told we can't do it. I've been told to shut my mouth! Let me tell you something: I have resolved to be the best me by not living in those past spaces.

Instead, I am trucking for Jesus, and I'm taking the steps that He has given me to take. I can't do it for you. You can whine all you want. You've been hurt; I get it. I have had leaders in my life write me letters containing things like, "Well, who would ever have thought that you could do this?" I could be discouraged by such letters. But I made a choice to be challenged by those letters.

Have you heard the expression *squat and watch*? Tell me I can't do something. Go ahead, tell me. Just say, "You can't do it." And God will laugh and help me do it. The same applies to you. Forget the past. Forget what others have said or continue to say. God has helped me in these kinds of times. If you tell me we cannot take a church that is ten percent of what it was and do anything new with it, I will go back to God. From my experiences, I've learned and I believe God will have something to show you. If you tell me we cannot move a church into a new season—even a declining church where the leaders who are still there say we should close the doors—then again, because of my experience, I believe God will have something to say. Here is what I know: "It ain't over until the horizontally enhanced lady sings" is just *not true*. Friend, it ain't over *until God says so*.

So if the Church is Jesus's bride, we are not going to simply shut it down. I don't get those who say otherwise. Their pasts and their assumptions are making God too small. Don't be like people who make God too small.

At the first place I worked, the children's pastor said some things to me. Somehow, I had made him mad, and to this day, I don't know how, but boy, was he mad. It seemed as if, in his anger, he convinced the whole church to hate me too. You know what I did? I knelt down in front of him and his group of leaders, and I apologized for whatever I have done. I asked him to forgive me. There was nothing else I could do, so I knew I had to handle it the only way I knew how—the right way. I didn't want my Nexts to be affected by my past.

Then, there was the church that fired me because they didn't have enough money to pay me, and then they asked me to get out of town. The pastor took this course of action because he thought I wanted his job—to be the pastor of this church where he was struggling. I didn't want that at all. I was a young youth pastor; I knew I only had a few years' experience. How could I have taken a dying church and turned it around? I was trying to figure out how to be a youth pastor at that time. But in his mind, that was what was happening. He reported his beliefs to our state leadership. Oh, my . . . you want to talk about hurt? I can keep going. How far do you want me to dig this hole? My point is this: No matter how badly you have been hurt, somebody has gone through what you did with a fever. All of us have been hurt, but ain't nobody been hurt like Jesus.

JESUS'S NEXT NEXTS LED TO THE ULTIMATE NEXT

Jesus has multiple Nexts ahead of his big Next, didn't he? His creation rejected him; his nation rejected him; his family called him demon-possessed and rejected him; his own disciples left him—one denied him three times but not before another betrayed him—and his closest friend ran from him in his most trying moments. When he was hanging on the cross, experiencing separation from the Father—when he cried out, "My God, My God, why have you forsaken me?" (Matthew 27:46, NIV) . . . that is the ultimate Next. But there was a road to get even there, wasn't there?

Talk about rejection. Can you imagine the pain Jesus felt at that moment when God turned his face? Years of my pain will never compare. So I am going to tell you right now; buckle up, soldier. Let Jesus set you free from the pain. The enemy is trying to keep it in your life. The enemy is trying to keep you bound by the pain of your past. The enemy will even surround you with people that have similar pain to remind you of your painful past. Do not blame God for it anymore. You hold the key to freedom in your servant's heart, and if you don't open the door to God's call . . . well, then you are going to stay where you are, my friends.

If you release your pain, your past, to God, and you get out of your now and into the Next that God has for you, your life will be radically different. You will come alive like never before. It will be like coming from death to life. It will be a resurrection for you. A new life. You will find freedom like you have never known. You will find opportunities you've never had before. All of the things you have prayed for but didn't feel as if you could get through to God because of the pain you are holding—it will be over and gone. You will have freedom. You will have a direct connection to God, and you will move when He moves you. It will be glorious.

SUMMARY

Next is not about getting to the end, but about getting to your now. Our Nexts are now. I don't know what your Next is, and I don't know where your next is. I do know *when* your Next is. It's right now. It's taking the next step and finding your quarter, putting it in the game of life, and trusting Jesus to lead you faithfully and lovingly. It is finding the moments God creates to step into your Next and then letting him take you to every Next after that. Your Next is within your God encounters.

Are you ready to take your first step, your Next step? Are you ready to put the past behind you and never give up?

Father, give us the courage to step to our Next, which is your now. Because we know our Next is now. You pulled me away in solitude for days. It's not easy for me, but Jesus, I commit to you—I committed to you there and I commit to you again—with and for my friends. I'm stepping to my Next. I'm asking You to help them step to theirs. Right now. In Jesus's name . . .

If you are willing to step into your Next, I am asking you to put this book aside for a few moments and make an altar right where you are. I pray (as I write this paragraph) that you will have your own burning bush encounter. This experience might just set up your life for months or years to come. It could set you on a journey of Nexts, which only God can connect to form your divine journey. I pray for you to hear with clarity the voice of God. I pray for you as you enter the Holy of Holies. Step into your Next. Jesus, here we are, take us in! The fire is burning in the holy place. The bush is on fire; let's step to it and not walk by it. Listen, His voice is calling from the fire. Take your first step. When you get to your altar, just listen for His voice. Speak to Him. If you need to lay some things before Him, surrender your past and your now. Step into His now, your Next.

6

AMAZING IS
JUST AHEAD

The journey to Next is divine; consecrate yourself!

When I transitioned from youth ministry to the lead pastor role, I felt as though I was out of my league, working in a different wheelhouse. I felt I had not really trained for this new phase of ministry. I had developed a life of prayer and meditated on His Word before this Next, but I knew I had to dive in much deeper to navigate this new season.

I read how fervently some great lead pastors prayed and studied, and I developed a deeper life of consecration. I spent early mornings in prayer and dove into Bible meditations for everyday ministry, then engaged in weekend and evening prayer for the weekend ministry. God met with me personally in so many amazing ways.

The most incredible thing God did in this season was in the ministry of the church I served. The services were life-changing! The outreaches were harvesting lives from the community where we served. And the church family was engaged at an all-time high in serving within the church and in the community. Family and children's programs were growing at incredible rates. The mission's program was exponentially transforming. Financial giving increased in generous ways. We added a family life building that served our church and community. We experienced a revival in multiple layers.

Just to be clear, this wasn't my doing. I faced some difficult times during this same season. Some leaders rebelled, even backslid in their faith. Other leaders attacked my leadership, and some leaders left. A few leaders stopped supporting the ministry, while others challenged everything we did.

But I also had influential leaders who served alongside me and supported our efforts. They were amazing men and women of God who had a solid yet growing faith. They trusted God and believed in me. And I'll be forever grateful.

This season of dependence on God came in two parts: I journeyed into the Next path God had for me; and then I journeyed with God in that Next, keeping pace with Him, and not moving ahead too fast or falling behind in doubt and fear.

Psalm 37:23 says, "The Lord directs the steps of the godly; He delights in every detail of their lives. Though they stumble they will never fall down for the Lord holds them by the hand." If you are a Christ-follower, you should say, *the Lord's got my hand*. And know He's got it no matter what.

JOSHUA'S TURN

With every step you take, God's already there. You can step without Him, you can step around Him, you can step away from Him, but if you are going to step with Him, you have to know God has your Next. Remember, those quarters still have the phrase *In God We Trust* on them. I trust God with my Next, no matter how hard it is. You should too.

Let's look at Joshua 3:5: "Consecrate yourselves for tomorrow the Lord will do amazing things among you." We are fast-forwarding the storyline from Moses to Joshua. On your DVDs (do people still own those?), DVRs, TVs, or music players, you can find some type of fast-forward button that enables you to move forward to another part of the movie or a different song. Do you ever wish you could fast-forward parts of your life too?

Maybe you are about to have a colonoscopy and you wish you could fast-forward through all the prep work and the procedure just to get to the good news from the doctor that you are clean and clear. The times most of us really want to fast-forward are when we face the challenging seasons in our lives. We think, *Let's move it on so I get past this moment!*

What I have learned is that in every season or moment that I am going through, God is taking me by the hand and teaching me something. To be transparent, there are some times when He teaches me that I wish I could reach for the fast-forward button and ask God if can we jump ahead. The problem with fast-forwarding is we miss parts of what God is trying to teach us.

It would take me books to tell you all the steps through Moses's journey. For now, I will fast-forward to the beginning of Joshua's leadership season to get the Israelites to the Promised Land. Joshua, Moses's successor, took the mantle of leadership with this challenge: *"Consecrate yourselves for tomorrow the Lord will do amazing things among you* (Joshua 3:5).

To understand where we are going, we have to remember where we have come from. With these memories, we recall the lessons we have learned in each Next we have traveled. We remember the places we have been, the lessons we have learned, and His presence, which we have experienced. All of these moments of Next serve to propel us into our next Next. We can celebrate every moment, every amazing experience, and connect the dots to see not only where God has brought us, but also where He may take us.

THE PATTERN OF 40-40-40

The Next God is taking us into is an amazing Next that's yet to be seen—but by God Himself. In the life of Moses, the pattern was 40-40-40. Moses was forty years old when he stepped out to try on the shoes that God had for him when he tried to step into his first Next. Remember, Moses was trying to determine his destiny and his destination. If God has a Promised Land for you, you don't want to stay in Egypt any longer than you have to. Egypt is symbolic in the Old Testament and represents sin and slavery. We want to get to the land of promises that God has for us.

We know where we are, but we want to get to where we're going. We don't want to stay where we are—eating porridge and making bricks for the rest of our lives—we want to move into the land flowing with milk and honey, a land running over with provision. Moses, at forty, assumes some leadership role with an attempt at conflict management but gets it all wrong. Then Moses hits another forty. Forty years on the backside of the desert. In this forty, he has leadership lessons to learn as a shepherd. He would learn to lead people by leading sheep. You know God calls us sheep.

Have you ever worked with sheep? I've worked with other farm or ranch animals but not sheep. It is my understanding, though, that they do not always smell very pleasant. Most of the time, you have to help them get where you want them to go. You have to guide them and guard them along the journey. You have to care for them when they are hurt. They will wander aimlessly and even get themselves into danger. Jesus calls us sheep, and we can be just like them in the behavioral aspects, especially with wandering, wondering, and wandering again about where we're going. Wondering how we are going to get there, wondering where we have been. Wondering how long this is going to take to get there. Knowing that God has a place, a purpose, a plan, a timing, and steps to get there is helpful.

The hope is found in knowing that the steps of a righteous person are ordered by the Lord. And the steps lead to something amazing. That's the promise. He's got a land of promise to get us to. When we can't step into our destiny or get to our destination, God will take us to the back side of the desert to teach us what we need to know, even if it takes another forty years.

40-40-40.

In the first forty, Moses is forty years old and steps out. The second forty is his learning period at "Sheep University," and his final forty starts in the classroom of the burning bush and turns into Moses returning to lead the people out of Egypt, with a detour in the wilderness.

The last forty is not about Moses. The last portion of the last forty is about the people. They cried and cried and cried and cried (you get the picture) for God to deliver them and help them get out of slavery, but then moaned about the wilderness, taking the detours God knew they needed. Finally, they get to the edge of the Promised Land, the land flowing with milk and honey. (One little guy in one of my services where I was helping the kids understand the phrase, "a land flowing with milk and honey," said it would have been better to say, "a land flowing with chicken and rice." Another shouted out, "a land flowing with chicken and waffles!" Basically, it means the *provision of God.* There is provision in His promise.

JUST ONE MORE

Moses sends out the spies to stake out the land to conquer it. Remember, God promised it was theirs. He promised he would go before them. He would equip them to take what He was giving them. Well, many of the spies—most of them—came back and reported, "We can't do it. We are like grasshoppers in their eyes."

Here is a question I have always wondered: Did they interview the "ites" families? The Amalekites, the Hittites, the Jebusites, the Amorites, and the Canaanites" Did the interview any of them? Did they ask them, "What do we look like to you?" Was the answer grasshoppers? As spies, it's doubtful they did any interviews of any type. What they reported was their own perception of themselves. They didn't even know what the truth was.

We find out later there was fear among the people living in the land about the Israelites coming to take the land. Fear doesn't see the Israelites like grasshoppers. Fear by those who lived in the Promised Land would mean they saw the Israelites as conquerors. Yet the spies reported that the "ites" were big people. They had big weapons; they had big cities.

Two spies were different. Joshua and Caleb. They encouraged the Israelites with, "We are well able to conquer them! It is not about our size; it is about God's size and whose side we are on. We don't need to tell God how big our challenge is; we need to tell our challenge how big our God is!"

Where two or three are gathered in His name, God is with them. When God is with you, there isn't anything that you cannot accomplish for Him. God opens doors that man cannot close and closes doors that man cannot open. I look at it this way: I just need one more. I need a Caleb or a Joshua with me on any day to run with me, to take us to the Promised Land that God has promised to give us. Someone to go in with me, to scatter the inhabitants of the land, and to empower us to take the land. I only need one Caleb or Joshua who will go with me to influence the rest of the Church family to be who God called us to be.

THE POWER OF BELIEF

God may look to send you through your next forty. Maybe you've been through the first forty to get started. Maybe you've been through the middle forty and learned a few things along the way. You don't want to know what happens to Moses in his last forty. When they got to the edge of the land, and all of the people believe the fearful majority rather than the God-empowered minority—Caleb and Joshua—they determined they couldn't proceed because, in their eyes, they are grasshoppers. Moses said, on behalf of God, "Then you don't get the land of promise because you don't believe."

The Israelites are sent back out into the desert for another forty years—Moses's last forty. It wasn't about what they did or didn't do; it wasn't about how much they gave or didn't give in the offering plates; it wasn't about how they did or did not worship. It was because they chose not to believe in God's promise. If you don't believe in His promise, you won't receive His promise. Hebrews 3:19 says, "They did not enter their rest because of their unbelief."

Belief in biblical terms, compared to our concept of belief, is about trust. Our worldly belief is like Disney World-type imagination; we play make-believe, or we have a fake-till-we-make-it kind of belief. Yet *to believe* in the Old and the New Testament is a trust that carries with it not only an understanding and appreciation of God's sovereignty but also carries action. It's a belief that causes us to move because we believe. I can say (all day even), "I believe, I believe, I believe," but it's going to take trusting action from me to move my feet in my faith.

When His Word says that if we believe in the Lord, Jesus Christ, we shall be saved, it's not mental assent. If it was just mental assent, demons could be saved, for the Bible says, ". . . even the demons believe this . . ." that He exists, "and they tremble in terror" (James 2:19). Belief is about mental assent that ignites a heart's passion, which moves feet into action—to get us to where God wants us to go, doing what God wants us to do, and being who God wants us to be.

During Moses's last forty, everyone over the age of twenty-one died in the desert (except Joshua and Caleb). Do you know why all those people died in the desert? It's not because they didn't like the worship, not because they didn't like the preacher; it's because they didn't believe. They didn't really trust God when He said He had come to rescue them.

There will come a moment in our lives when He will take us to the edge of our own land of promise and look for us to take that step into our Next. When we take that step in, He will meet us there. We will see rivers open us for us to cross and fortified, seemingly impenetrable walls fall down, cities surrender, enemies run from us. And we should keep pursuing that Next until God gives us all He has promised.

All those adult Israelites were buried in the desert. Don't get buried in your unbelief. Don't let bugs eat your body because you would not believe in His promise. Be a believer, one who is led to milk and honey, safe in a home you did not have to build, living in a well-provisioned land.

MY BELIEF ABOUT YOUR NEXT

I believe God is going to reveal His personal plan for your life. I believe He is going to reveal Himself to you. I believe He is going to light up your feet on your path. I believe He is ordering your steps. I believe He is interested in every detail, every day of your life. I believe God has got your Next. I believe God did not make a mistake with you. I believe God will equip you and empower you for every next Next. I believe you are not alone. I believe God chose you. I believe you are the head and not the tail. I believe you are His child. I believe God heard me when I prayed all these prayers over all who read them . . . so receive them, my friend.

If you are twenty-one or younger, I am one of your greatest believers. I believe in you and what God will do in and through you. I will not abdicate my responsibility by allowing you to go to the Promised Land by yourself. I will not let you have to figure it out alone because I'm too faithless to believe. I will not let you try to make it on your own because you did not have anyone to lead the way or show you the way. I will not let you be left alone in the desert. You will not have to get a shovel and bury me in the desert. We are going together into the Promised Land, into our Nexts.

You should tell those over twenty-one that you need them. Joshua 3:5 was written to everyone younger than twenty-one, preparing them to take the Promised Land, when they were sixty-one and under—forty years later. Joshua speaks to the crowd: "Moses my servant is dead." Joshua was already anointed to be the successor to Moses. Joshua was chosen by Moses and God. Do you know why Joshua was qualified to be the new leader? He certainly did not have the training Moses had—Moses had been raised in the king's household in Egypt. Joshua served Moses. He attended to Moses. He constantly and consistently served Moses. He washed Moses's hands. When Moses would meet with God in all His glory in the tent of meeting, Joshua would be right there with Moses in the tent and would stay after Moses walked out, just to be in the presence of the Lord. God needs people to lead who are passionate about being in His presence. Joshua, at the Lord's command and in his experience, says *consecrate yourself, for tomorrow the Lord will do amazing things.*

Consecrate means to set apart, make holy, sanctify, and prepare something. When God said *consecrate*, He was talking about all of that. Set yourself apart. Make yourself holy; sanctify yourself, and prepare yourself for God's Next for your life, for tomorrow, the Lord will do amazing things among us. A holy God is about to do amazing things among us. A prepared God is about to do amazing things He's prepared among us. So the only way to receive the prepared, holy, and amazing things He has is to consecrate ourselves.

We do not have to create the amazing Nexts ourselves. If we created them, they wouldn't come close to matching His kind of amazing. As a pastor, I want you to experience the amazing God has for you so much that I could try to create amazing, anointed, or powerful Nexts for you. But my man-created amazing would never get close to God's amazing. If you are a pastor or leader, join me, and let's help others by modeling what it is to consecrate themselves. Let's give room for God to take care of the amazing. God is in the creation business; God is in the redemption business, and God is in the *making all things new* business. God is in the healing business; God is in the way-making business, God is in the Next business, and God is in the whosoever-will business. God is in the Promised Land business. And I, as a pastor and leader, am in the servanthood business, foot-washing business, and loving and testifying businesses. I will leave the amazing to Him! God will bring the amazing to our tomorrows.

I encourage you to take some time today, right after you finish reading this chapter, and spend that time in consecration with the Lord. Surrender yourself, every part and portion, inside and out. Submit to His Lordship. As the old-timers might say, get it all under the blood of Jesus. Consecrating ourselves should be at the top of our "to do" or "to be" lists. Just to be clear: if we invert this passage, there will be no amazing without consecration.

Consecrating ourselves is our worship and active faith. It is worship because we consecrate ourselves in honor of who He is. It is faith in action because we act in obedience, regardless if amazing comes or not. However, His Word is true, and the Bible is recorded and written for us, to reveal God to us in all His glory and character, and for us to know how God works and interacts with His creation (that's us). Therefore, as we activate our lives full of faith, consecrating ourselves, He will create amazing Nexts among us.

THE HOLY NEXTS

Does The New Covenant (The New Testament) have anything to say about our part in God's Nexts for our lives? Hebrews 12:14: "Work at living in peace with everyone, and work at living a holy life . . ." This is a command that includes an implied "you." You and I have to go to work. I'm not talking about your nine-to-five job. I'm talking about we've got to get to work at living a holy life. A consecrated life in Joshua. The words *holy* and *consecrated* are used interchangeably at time times in the Old Testament, both meaning *to be separated, set apart*. Living a *holy life*.

Look at the next part of that Scripture: ". . . for those who are not holy will not see the Lord." Without holiness, we ain't seeing the Promised Land. If you don't consecrate yourself, you will not see the amazing Next God has for you.

Not only are we to be set apart for God, but we are also to be set apart from sin. God is looking for a genuine relationship, and we can't have this if we're mired in sin. He's not looking at how you believe you are living; He is looking at how you *really are* living. The intimate relationship He is looking for is separated from sin and unto Him.

Some people may want to keep a little sin in their pockets yet still get close to God at the same time. If that is you, then you do not understand the requirement of a holy God. A holy God will not shack up with sin. That's bad, isn't it? Hold on. I'm going to get you there. The words *holy* and *consecration* are used over 600 times in the Old and New Testaments. How many times did your mama or daddy repeat a command before you responded like you should have responded? When my momma told me to do something, sometime I wouldn't respond until she said it three times. With my daddy . . . it was zero times. My daddy just gave me "the look." I didn't try to get out of it. If momma said something, I could ease around it about three times before I'd get what I deserved for my lack of respect or slow response times. So if *God* says something 600 times, you better believe it is important, valuable. Old and New Testament: *Be holy, consecrate yourself. Be holy as I am holy.*

We can set ourselves apart or consecrate our lives by doing these three things:

> *1.) We can do it by seeing sin as an offense to a holy God, not just personal defeat.*

There are many people who simply view sin as mistakes—*well, I blew it this time.* They don't truly recognize that they offended God. David, when it was brought to his attention that he messed up with Bathsheba, knew he had offended God. If you want to have a revelation of what it is like to know you have offended God with your sin, read what David wrote in Psalm 51. He asks God not to take His Holy Spirit from him. It is the picture of true repentance.

> *2.) We can be set apart or consecrate our lives by taking responsibility for our actions and our sins while depending on the grace of God to help us.*

At times, we may feel like we can't seem to win our sin battles. Listen, my friend, God gives you the grace to win. If you try to defeat it by yourself, you will be defeated. If you will take hold of His hand, He'll lead you to a place called *obedience*, which will lead you to victory.

> *3.) We can be set apart or consecrate our lives by obeying God in all areas of our lives, even in the seemingly insignificant ones.*

He said He will order every step and is interested in every detail of our lives. We cannot enjoy His interest in every detail of our lives if we are not willing to surrender every detail of our lives to Him. We have these insignificant areas, areas we think God will let something go. That these pockets of sin aren't as important as other, *bigger* sins. Know this: It's the little foxes that spoil the vine. In other words, all of the little, insignificant areas add up fast to overwhelm us. In the New Testament book of James, Jesus's brother tells us when the little sins grow up, they will kill us spiritually. For without holiness (separation from the rule and reign of the unholy, we will not see the Lord now or later) and if we are still ruled and reigned by the unholy (Egypt), we will never see our Promised Land.

VICTORY IN OUR NEXTS

Some of us are so interested in victory, we forget obedience is what God is looking for from us. Real victory is obedience within the Kingdom of God. Often, people just want the victory; they gotta have the victory. I get it. I have a competitive nature too. I want to win as much or more than the next guy or gal. But if all I am looking for is the win, it's a personal thing. It's all about me. But if I am looking to obey, that is a God thing. Obedience will give us the Kingdom victory we crave because God does not lose.

On the flip side, we are not set apart or consecrated if we settle for mediocrity. When we consecrate ourselves, we don't consecrate ourselves for the leftovers. I like leftovers as much as the next person, but they just are not the same as when they are piping hot and just out of the oven. I don't stop at Krispy Kreme to get the day-old doughnuts. I stop at Krispy Kreme because the red sign is illuminated, and it reads "Hot and Ready." When I put the doughnut in my mouth and it touches my tongue, I want the heat from the vat it was just fried in to warm me up. I want that white creamy sugar frosting to still be in its thick liquid form, not its cold, crusted form that flakes off. I am not settling for day-old doughnuts.

I will buy a little coffee from the corner gas station, but I am not buying the day-old Krispy Kreme when I can drive a few more blocks where another "Hot and Ready" sign is lit up in the window.

How much more do we, as the children of God, settle for mediocrity? We will just pull up to life any old time and want it any old way. God did not call us to consecration to settle for mediocrity. There is amazing waiting for us. We were set apart to hit the mark, not miss the mark. Another definition of sin is missing the mark. The mark or the target bullseye is God's plan for our lives. God has the very best for us. He wants us to reach our Next, our Promised Land, one that He has had ready for us for a long time. We will not settle for mediocrity in our lives. God sets us apart from the realm and rule of sin. He empowers us to resist sin. We must choose to resist anything less than our amazing Next.

If I asked you about any sporting event and who came in second place, I bet most of us couldn't remember. Who won the silver medal? Who lost the World Series? Who lost the NBA or WNBA Championships? Who lost the NCAA March Madness Championship? It's always harder to remember who lost. Why? There's something about hitting the mark that is memorable. There's something about getting where you wanted to go. God has made a Promised Land for his people that may be sitting out there, like a ghost town, because His people are settling for everything else except what God has promised them. We have a responsibility: Don't settle for mediocrity. The struggle is real.

Paul said it like this: "So I find this law at work: Although I want to do good, evil is right there with me. For in my inner being I delight in God's law; but I see another law at work in me, waging war against the law of my mind and making me a prisoner of the law of sin at work within me. What a wretched man I am! Who will rescue me from this body that is subject to death? Thanks be to God, who delivers me through Jesus Christ our Lord!" (Romans 7:21–25, NIV).

Yes, the struggle is real. For everyone. When Paul asks *who will rescue me* in his struggle, he answered with the same one who said He would rescue the Israelites from Egypt: Jesus Christ my Lord and Savior, and He will take me to the Promised Land!

The Apostle Peter struggled too. He said it like this: But just as he who called you is holy, so be holy in all you do; for it is written: "Be holy, because I am holy" (1 Peter 1:15, NIV). Let me define the word *all* for you in the Greek. (The New Testament is originally written in Greek.) You might want to write this definition in your journal. *All* in the Greek—and in this passage—means "all." It is the total sum of everything. Nothing is left out. All of me—in mind, body, and spirit— should be holy. There is an amazing Next waiting on me to consecrate my complete self.

Here are three practical things we must do to consecrate ourselves.

1.) We must pray.

Pastor, I do pray, you might say. I know. "Now I lay me down to sleep; I pray thee, Lord, my soul to keep." I will take it if that's all you have, but I think you've got more in you. Maybe you can pray as the amazing Savior taught us:

Our Father, which art in Heaven, Holy is your name. Your Kingdom come, Your will be done on earth as it is in Heaven. Give us today our daily bread. Forgive us our debts as we forgive our debtors. Lead us not into temptation, deliver us from evil. For yours is the kingdom, power and the glory, forever. Amen (Matthew 6:9).

If you pray this prayer three times a day, you will be amazed at what God will do in your life. Prayer is holding God by His hand. If you are holding His hand, you are close to Him. If you are holding His hand, you are moving with Him. If you are holding His Hand, you are feeling the warmth, love, and protection He offers. If you are holding His hand, you may be feeling the pulsing of His heartbeat, which beats for you. If you are holding His hand, you are going where He is going and doing what He is doing, and you are being what He is being.

Prayer, like Jesus taught us, aligns us with Him. The prayer begins with "Our Father.". It's relational; He's the Father, and we are the kids. He's "our" Father. This positions us for a very personal conversation with God. He is established as our Father "in Heaven," a place we consider the house of our supreme authority (because it does). Authority trumps power every time. Authority has power at its command. So our Father has supreme authority over every entity known to us.

So "our Father who is in heaven" should receive the honor due to Him at the beginning of all of our conversations with Him. "Holy is your name" is a great start. The proclamation, declaration, and adoration that we give Him continue to align us with Him. The worship we offer should be worthy of who He is. He is looking for true worshippers, those who worship Him in Spirit and in truth.

The primary petition in this prayer is not for our needs and wants to be met. It is to align us with His plans and purposes or His path for our steps. *Your Kingdom come, Your will be done on earth as it is in heaven.* If we are pursuing the steps that He has ordered for us, our Nexts, then we are anticipating His Kingdom to come and His will to be done. This is His victory. This Next is not what we are trying to manipulate Him with; it is us aligning with the steps He has ordered as if they are ordered in and for Heaven.

The rest of the prayer includes provision and daily dependence (*Give us today our daily bread*); righteousness and surrender (*Forgive us our debts as we forgive our debtors*); submission to His holy leadership (*Lead us not into temptation*); protection in His power (*deliver us from evil*); and recognition of His authority (*For yours is the kingdom, power and the glory, forever*). Each of these components continues to align us with the steps He is ordering for us. This powerful prayer of alignment will lead us to our Next in Him. To victory.

2.) We must prepare ourselves by reading, knowing, and using the Word.

His Word is a lamp to our feet and a light for our paths. We don't have to worry about losing our way, running into anything, falling off a cliff, or stubbing our toes on something because we have the Word—the lamp to our feet and a light for our path on the steps the Lord has ordered for us. When we don't have that Word, we're walking in dark places. Without the Word, we live in frustration and aggravation and agitation. With the Word, we live in illumination, liberation, and celebration.

The pathway to our Nexts may be unfamiliar. In many cases, they may be unknown to us. We have not traveled this way before. We may not know the turns, the landmarks, or the distances. His Word, as the lamp and light, will amazingly guide us in the journey. The consistency of reading the Word seems to keep us on His path.

Through the years, I have enjoyed being outdoors: walking, hiking, hunting, fishing, camping, and more. I have traveled through woods, deserts, mountains, valleys, and even cities. Travel is always easier when there are well-marked pathways, especially when there are multiple paths that could confuse the journey. Some of this travel has been at night. The darker it is—because of clouds, little or no moonlight, or large trees or bushes blocking the light—the more challenging it is to stay on the path. It is amazing what a flashlight can do to bring peace and help on a journey. The Word is God is the light that will keep you on His path every day, every step along the way. Neglected time in the Word can cost you more time than necessary, result in bigger challenges on the trip, and even open the door for unnecessary pain or injury. Knowing all that, turn on your light; read His word daily. Find a systematic Bible reading plan and stay with it.

As you read His Word, you will be reminded about the steps to your Next:

> Psalm 17:5, *My steps have held to your paths; my feet have not stumbled.*

> Psalm 119:59, *I have considered my ways and have turned my steps to your statutes.*

> Proverbs 16:9, *In their hearts humans plan their course, but the* Lord *establishes their steps.*

> *3.) We must prepare ourselves by following His direction.*

The Lord directs the steps of the godly; he delights in every detail of their lives. He directs. Have you ever been in a traffic situation where an officer directed the traffic? Have you ever not obeyed the directions the officer gave you? There is usually a valuable reason for the officer giving those directions. The directions are likely for everyone's safety. The directions are for protection. The directions may be for provision. Maybe the road was washed out; there was an accident ahead, a boulder was knocked loose, there was a fire, or there was an ongoing, life-threatening crime. I have been directed and redirected because of all of these situations and more.

Isn't it amazing we take directions from people better than we take directions from God? Yet God has promised to direct every step with love and cares about every detail of our process. There is nobody on earth that cares for you like God does. There is nobody on earth that has ever provided for you like He has and will. We have never been treated as well as God treats us by anybody on this earth. We have to prepare ourselves, consecrate ourselves by following the directions God gives us. *Be holy, for I am holy.* God has amazing Nexts waiting on us!

He declares in His word that He will give us the direction we need to our Nexts:

Proverbs 20:24, *A person's steps are directed by the LORD.*

Jeremiah 10:23, *LORD, I know that people's lives are not their own; it is not for them to direct their steps.*

1 Peter 2:21 (emphasis mine), ***To this you were called****, because Christ suffered for you, leaving you an example, **that you should follow in his steps***.

Some of Jesus's first words to Peter and a few of the other disciples were also some of His last words to them. Jesus told them, "Come, follow me, and I will make you a fisher of men." The call was to follow Him into the new Next for them. The Bible tells us, "Immediately, they dropped their nets and followed Him." Following His directions and call it is necessary to get to the new Next. Expect the "new" next to feel awkward and even uncomfortable because you have never gone that way before or done that thing before. If He calls you to the new Next, then follow Him. Follow His directions. He's got you.

At a beach, over breakfast, Jesus calls to Peter again, "Follow me" (John 21:19, 22). When we get off path, say bad things, and even run the other way, Jesus will meet with us to redirect our steps and get us to our Next anyway, just like He did with Peter. He knows what we will do as we give in to doubt and temptation. Yet He still keeps pursuing us to get us to our Next in Him.

> Give me a minute here: *Thank you, Jesus, for Your grace, patience, and mercy for me. Thanks for Your continued persistence in Your pursuit of me. Thank You for Your love for me, even when I am not very loveable. You are amazing, Jesus. I love You and hope in You!*

As I was writing these words, I once again realized how gracious Jesus is to me (and you) and wanted to stop and give Him some praise. You see, I'm living this as I am writing it. I believe I will live this as long as I am living here, in this lifetime. And I am confident He has my Nexts. Every one of them.

Remember what He said: *Though they stumble, they will never fall, for the Lord holds them by the hand* (Psalm 37:23). So no matter where you are in your journey, He's got your Next, and it will be amazing!

7

EVERY NEXT PATH
HAS A PACE

"Since we live by the Spirit, let us keep in step with the Spirit"
(Galatians 5:25).

S tepping, or step-dancing, is a rhythmic dance in which the participants' entire bodies are used as instruments to produce complex sounds through a mixture of footsteps, spoken words, and handclaps. I don't know if you have ever seen or participated in a great "step team." Well, a superb step team is a cool thing to witness or be a part of. I love watching students do this because they'll step in sequence to a specific beat. And it all communicates a story of unity and power. And look—I think you're either good at it, or you're not. And I don't know if there is anywhere in between.

We've learned that the journey of Next is about stepping—in a unified, powerful pace that is set by the rhythm of the Holy Spirit. The Bible says the Lord determines our steps, yet Galatians 5:25 also says, "Since we live by the Spirit, let us keep in step with the Spirit."

Now that term, *in step,* in the Greek language is a military term that would have been used to set the line in order. If you've been in the military, you understand what they're talking about. In basic training, they start you right off by lining up correctly, in sync. They want you to "dress right dress." They want you to be "right" in every alignment and step. They want you to be on pace. Not only will they line you up, but also, they get you on the right path. Then they're going to keep you at the same pace. So they'll say things like this, "Left, left, left, right, left" because they want you at the same pace as everyone around you.

If you've been in a marching band, you might know it goes about the same way. You have a drummer, or drum major, who gives you the cadence or rhythm for the pace of the marching. The band has to move in rhythm, on pace, even when there is no music.

There's something about not only the path of our Nexts but the pace of our Nexts that keeps us in step with the Spirit as we journey on our paths. I believe that is what Paul is speaking about when he refers to living by the Spirit; we must keep in step with Him. Not only is there a path to follow (that's lit, as we learned earlier), but there is a pace to keep. If we don't keep the pace, we're going to either be ahead of Him or behind Him. Or we're going to be completely off the path He created for us. We've got to keep pace with the Spirit.

The Holy Spirit in the New Testament is the represented manifest presence of God, just as the "glory of God" was the manifest presence for the Israelites and the Ark of the Covenant in the Old Testament. In the Old Testament, whenever the Ark was there, so was the manifest presence of God. He would often be like a fog, called a *kabod*—a glory of God. The glory of God was said to have a weighty feeling about Him, and it would be so strong that sometimes in the temple, the priest could not even complete their ministry.

In the New Testament, it is still possible for God to manifest Himself in similar ways. God sends the Holy Spirit to be the manifest presence of God. The Holy Spirit dwells within us (if you're a believer) and doesn't just visit us now and then. He takes up residence in our lives when we have a relationship with the Father through Jesus, and He will empower us as a resident in our lives. Christ-followers in pursuit of our Nexts, we want to look at how the Holy Spirit wants to keep us in step. The Holy Spirit, the manifest presence of God, sets the path and the pace for the followers of Jesus Christ.

THE OWNER OF THE PACE

When we have the Holy Spirit living and at work in our lives, we can find the path and pace for moving to our

Next. Many "church people" usually get excited about certain things—attendance, for example. We get excited when people show up (including ourselves). When we get to church and check off that "to do" item called "church attendance," we feel like we've arrived because we've been physically present. I'm a big proponent of gathering together for church, prayer, worship, and serving. I'm also a big proponent of being excited about everything we do. Showing up is not all there is.

There's nothing wrong with getting excited about these things, but there's more to consider. I want you to understand that these types of things deal with us and our perspectives, not necessarily God's perspective. We look at the exterior acts of faith while God looks at the heart.

Some of us get excited about dressing up. You know, we want to look good and we're going to put on our best clothes or shoes or drive our best cars. We're going to do it right. We want to decorate everything "real pretty." We're going to weave it up. We're going to color it up. We tend to do everything we can to put on the airs of Christianity. Do you know what I'm talking about? But dressing up is not all there is, either.

We also get excited about how we start up—start something new. Have you ever had a New Year's resolution? Have you ever started a new workout plan? Have you ever started a new diet? Have you ever started a new discipline in your life? *Oh, I'm going to do something different this year.* I've heard that statement a thousand times, particularly in January of every year. Gyms sell more memberships and dealers more exercise equipment than in any other month out of the year. They need to quit calling it exercise equipment and call it clothes hangers because, after about thirty days, all most of us do is drape our clothes over them. All of the people who go to the gym year-round complain the gyms get crowded at the beginning of each year. They know it's coming every January. "Just wait," they say to each other, "by February or by March, the gym will be empty again." People don't follow through. They start up, but they don't finish. We get excited about the start-up, including church activities. And the next week, we don't show up. Nothing wrong with an exciting start-up, but that is not all there is.

Do you know the solution to all of this? We have to set a pace. That's going to get us stepping all the way to the finish line.

> **The Spirit of God is speaking to us, not just to show up, dress up, and start up but to pace up.**

If we don't pace up with the Holy Spirit, we can easily burn up and burn out before we cross the finish line.

We have to set a pace we can keep. The Holy Spirit knows what that pace is for each of us. I'm not just interested in anyone starting something they cannot finish. I'm interested in them completing what they've started. I'm interested in them finishing—at the finish line.

Sometimes, we want the Holy Spirit to let up, listen up, and line up. We want Him to do things our way when we get excited and start up. Sometimes in our zeal, we don't realize we tell the Holy Spirit to "Just hold on (let up); I got this. Just listen up. I got this. Let me show you how to do this." And then we want the Spirit to line up behind us and watch us. That is not at all how God explains we should follow Him.

Listen, fellow sojourners, we don't request that the Holy Spirit follow us. We follow Him. Are you with me? Come on, wake up! Look, before you get all upset with me, the Scriptures speak of leaders who struggled with the same things. Leaders like Moses, who fled to the desert after he tried to resolve conflict his way. We all have a tendency to want to do things our way. Many move for God, but they aren't able to finish. They hit a wall. They encountered some challenges, and they weren't able to finish what they had started.

I've known some people who get so excited about starting up, and they run their 5k or 10k, which is 3.1 miles or 6.2 miles, with no path or pace to success. They just start running. Well, after a few blocks, they are done.

My mother used to say it like this to me: "Your eyes are larger than your stomach." Have you ever heard that phrase? It was relative to eating because I would put so much food on my plate that I could not finish it. It is the same thing without a Holy Spirit pace. Our eyes get larger than our lives. We think, "Oh, I'm going to run ten miles a week" and end up running ten blocks. Come on now. We've got to set a pace with the help of the Holy Spirit so we know we can follow it—a pace that we can keep, a pace that we can use to finish.

A PACER AFTER GOD'S OWN HEART

David. A great king, shepherd, psalmist, worshipper, and leader. David had some pace issues as described in 2 Samuel 6 (also recorded in Chronicles.)

As I did with Moses, I want to share some of David's story with you. David decided it was time to bring the Ark of the Covenant, the manifest glory of God, back to Jerusalem. And that was a good thing. That was a righteous thing. It was the right thing to do.

The Ark had the stone tablets Moses received from God—the ones with The Ten Commandments etched in God's handwriting—and some other things in there that were precious to the Kingdom of God. Built on top of the ark were cherubim angels. This was the place where the glory would settle in the ministry times.

Previously, the Ark had been captured by the Philistines. However, they were having some real issues because they weren't the ones who were supposed to have it. You would have to go back and read the stories. Because the issues were so intense, the Philistines took the Ark and dropped it off near the border of Israel. It was placed at Abinadab's house. Abinadab's two sons were helping to take care of the cart the Ark was transported on; their names were Ahio and Uzzah. They had helped take care of it for several months. And then David said, it's time to bring it from the edge of the country, up the mountain, and to Jerusalem. (By the way, this is my way of telling the story.)

David calls a committee meeting—basically, a church business meeting. He says, "Are you guys with me? Do you think we ought to do this?" And every one of them said, "Yes, let's do this." And so they had a big parade. There was big, big fan fair. They lined all of the things up to receive the Ark back in Jerusalem. Everybody was ready. In fact, they had built a brand-new cart. This cart was the premier of carts. It probably had spinners on the hubcaps. You know, this cart probably had LED lights underneath. This cart was made from the best wood. It was the best-looking cart and probably had some powerful animals tied to the front end of it. All because David . . . well, he was a spender. He didn't mind making the best for the Lord, so he got the Cadillac Escalade model of carts.

This cart for the Ark had never been used before. And so it was an incredible thing David had done. Finally, they travel to the area where the Ark was kept to bring it back to the city. When the Ark was finally on the way, the oxen stumbled. They tripped! And when they tripped, Ahio was out in front of the cart. His job was to make sure the path was good and smooth. Uzzah is right beside the cart and the Ark, making sure the wheels were turning well. Suddenly, things happened so fast. Any of us would have had a similar reaction to the stumble. The oxen tripped, the Arc slid in the cart, and Uzzah had a purely reflexive response; he reached out and grabbed the Ark—which was a wooded box covered with gold on the inside and out.

Uzzah knew that if the Ark fell, the cherubim could easily break off the top. The Ark could easily crack on the sides or the lid. The tablets of stone inside could be further damaged. So Uzzah did what any of us would have done; he reached out to steady the Ark.

The problem was that God got angry. Scripture explains God was angry because Uzzah had touched the Ark, and Uzzah immediately died. God struck him down right there.

Then David grew angry. David was angry with God because Uzzah died. He had set up the whole parade. He had paid for the new cart to be built. But what God knew was that in David's heart, this amazing fanfare that David crafted was for himself. David thought he was doing things the "right way." Everything looked good, God-honoring for sure.

Excuse my rough language here, but David was ticked off at God. Not only was he mad, but David was also afraid. The Bible says both emotions came out. David said something like, "We can't take the Ark on up from here because who knows what God will do?" It is common for fear and anger to travel together. I've even heard that often anger is unresolved or unmanaged fear.

Then, David does something interesting. This had all happened near Obed-Edom's home. So David leaves the Ark with Obed-Edom. He doesn't take it to Jerusalem. He stops the parade. I mean, I get it. One of his key people in the parade had died. It is kind of hard to have a celebration when one guy dies in the middle of the party, especially when nobody understands the reason. They stayed at Obed-Edom's house for three months. As a result, everything Obed-Edom did was blessed. In ways no man could ever accomplish, Obed-Edom was blessed. It was unbelievable. And that's the whole story of 2 Samuel, Chapter 6.

Here's the challenge for us: David got mad when Uzzah died after touching the Ark because the oxen stumbled. Listen to me carefully. Your oxen are going to stumble some days. Your oxen may be stumbling right now. You don't want to trip over your oxen that are tripping.

So why would David get so angry with God? Why would God strike us down in the first place? What if we are just trying to honor and protect the prized possessions of God? What did Uzzah do wrong? If honoring and protecting the Ark was all this was about, David and Uzzah might have had a case to make, but that was not all it was about.

And David knew that. So did every Levite, including Uzzah and Ahio and their dad. They all knew the law. Being Israelites, they would have known the Torah, the first five books of the Bible. This is the place in the Bible where the commands to build, use, and protect the Ark are recorded. They knew what was required to move the Ark. The Ark—not just a box covered with gold—had rings on the four corners. The rings held the gold-covered poles, which extended through them, allowing people to lift the Ark and carry it from place to place. This meant those carrying the Ark on their shoulders would never touch it. Because it was holy. The Ark was never supposed to be put on an unholy cart to be transported. Rather, people lifted it onto their shoulders with the poles and carried the glory of the Lord. David knew this. But he ignored it.

Their argument held no water. "Well, the Philistines used a cart to transport the Ark." But the Philistines weren't the Israelites. They weren't God's Chosen people, and they didn't know the rules.

David built a cart, even though he knew the Ark's path and pace should never be on such a common thing as a cart. That's not all. Specifically, the Kohathites were to carry the Ark. Uzzah was from the tribe of Levi, but he wasn't Kohathite. And God was very clear that Kohathites were to be the ones who carried the Ark. That was their job. Nobody else could carry it.

Finally, the only Kohathite people who should touch the Ark were the priests. Uzzah was not a priest.

It was not just a matter of one guy doing something wrong. It was a litany of things that God had ordained, most of which were ignored. David had chosen a path and a pace to follow. And it wasn't God's.

There are three things from David's experience I want you to consider as we think about our pace:

1). In his anger and fear, David releases the Ark, the glory of God, to someone else. What emotions or circumstances might cause us to release what God has given us?

Emotions are part of the collection of gifts that God has given to each of us. They are helpful in many ways. We certainly don't want to be emotionless as we follow God. However, we do need to guard our minds and hearts. This is a command that God gives through many words: "Above all else, guard your heart, for everything you do flows from it" (Proverbs 4:23); "And the peace of God, which transcends all understanding, will guard your hearts and your minds in Christ Jesus" (Philippians 4:7).

> **We must learn to trust the King of our hearts, not the emotions in our hearts.**

We need to trust God over our emotions. I realize this thought will contradict most country songs and love ballads. But our emotions aren't worthy of trust. Listen as Jeremiah prophecies: "The human heart is the most deceitful of all things, and desperately wicked. Who really knows how bad it is? But I, the Lord, search all hearts and examine secret motives. I give all people their due rewards, according to what their actions deserve" (Jeremiah 17:9–10).

We have to ask ourselves, what is our price for the path and pace God has for us? What will we trade our Next for? What triggers and emotions can cause us to release the purpose and plan of God?

God help us stay resolute with Your grace.

2.) The second thing I learned from David in this story is this: He trades glory for a cart.

In the 1990s and 2000s, there was a buzzword that hit the Church world, which we've been living by ever since. Just to be clear, I am not opposed to it. But I hold it with caution. The word is *excellence*. We need to do everything with excellence. We need to do things at a higher level to honor God. That's true. But, also . . . that's what David did. When he built the cart, it was brand-new, top of the line. It was *excellent*.

Here is the challenge we have: when our excellence replaces His glory, we are always going to be in trouble with God. We can never allow a trade for His glory. I don't care how excellent what we do is; if it replaces the honor of the holiness of the glory of God, we put ourselves in jeopardy with Him. There's a path and a pace for us to follow. And it's not about how good the cart looks or how fancy the wheels are or that it has lights underneath. It's not about the oxen that pull it. **It's about the glory inside of it. It's about the glory on top of it. It's about the glory that goes everywhere it goes.** We cannot trade glory for a cart. We cannot trade the glory for excellence. Look, our churches are full of colorful lights, energetic music, and emotional services. Our churches have those services in fancy buildings, with detailed programs and expensive or intricate systems. None of these good things can ever replace the glory of God's presence. I think we ought to do it the best way we can to honor God. We should serve the best way we know how, but friends, we've got to look at the path and the pace of the Holy Spirit and make sure that our full attention and affection are for His glory.

3.) The third thing I learned from David's experience is a stumble can expose our weaknesses.

Yes, it was just a trip, instigated by the oxen who stepped in a hole. On rough terrain, on a rocky ascension up a mountain, an ox likely stumbles almost every time.

But it wasn't that stumble that defined the challenge. It was David's stumble. That became the challenge. He got angry, and it was an anger born of fear. Had David just followed the path and the pace of God, none of this would have happened because those carrying the Ark would have been Kohathites, shouldering the glory of God on their shoulders.

God is still looking for men and women who will put the glory on their shoulders. God is still looking for men and women who are listening to the Holy Spirit.

You know, in Revelation, the letters to all seven churches mentioned in Chapters 2 and 3 end with the same challenge. "He who has an ear, let him hear" what the Spirit is saying to the Church. Do you know why Jesus says that to all seven churches, even though two of them weren't doing anything wrong? He says it to them because they were not listening. I bet God may be saying it to us too.

EARS TO HEAR

Two of my children are now parents themselves. I often hear them (and their spouses) say to their children, "You're not being a good listener." Friends, we have to be good listeners. We have to be a good listener to the Holy Spirit who sets our pace as we pursue our Next paths. By the way, I wasn't as gentle as my grown children are with their kids. If they weren't listening, I would yell, "HEY! LISTEN TO ME!" I wasn't the best parent. The good news is that I got better as I got older. Thank God and my kids for grace! If they were not listening, I figured I needed to be louder. I did not think

I needed to teach them to listen better. My kids are trying to teach their kids to listen better. I think the Spirit of God, in those seven letters to the seven churches in Revelation, was trying to teach us to be better listeners. He who has an ear, let him hear what the Spirit is saying.

Why must we hear? To live the life He has for us. Because we must not only hear about the path, but we must hear about the pace. If we don't hear about the pace, we get ahead or we get behind Him—or we just choose our own way. We try to find that excellent way. But if we have ears to hear, we will find His beautiful way rather than a good-looking way. Rather than a way that everybody will be impressed with—except God, of course. We must get away from the temptation to say, "I can't wait to put this on social media. I can't wait to put it on our website. I can't wait to go to some conferences and speak about this to hundreds of people because everybody is going to say, 'Wow!'" We are challenged by the value we place on man's *wow* instead of on God's pleasure over our path and pace.

The Master's plan will prevail—eventually. We'll stumble and our weaknesses will be exposed, just like with David, who, remember, was a man after God's heart. During every Next journey we take, we are going to stumble; we are going to experience trips, and I don't mean the vacation kind.

When his weakness was exposed, it took David three months to figure it out. It may take us time to hear what the Spirit is saying to us. When David realized what he missed, he ordered them to get the poles, and they lifted the Ark onto their shoulders. Then, every so many feet, they stopped to worship God! They did this because David realized it wasn't the overall plan of bringing the Glory (the Ark) back to Jerusalem that was in question; it was the way he had overtaken it. The way he had overthrown God with his own plans. It was the pace David had set. So David slowed the pace and enhanced the journey with righteous worship!

Ladies, you may understand this first. Often, women say to us men, "It's not *what* you said."

We men say, "Huh? What did I say?"

The ladies reply, "It's *how* you said it." Women are trying to tell us it's the process, the attitude, and the position of our hearts that matter. The process is flawed. We need to find God's path—His process, His heart, and His pace—to stay on His path for our Nexts.

THE BEST QUESTION TO ASK

When we stumble, there is a best question to ask ourselves and others. What has my stumble or trip on this path to my Next revealed to me (individuals)? What have our church's stumbles or trips revealed to us (collectively)?

Is there anything our emotions have caused or lost us, things that God wanted us to have? What have we traded for Glory or the pace of the Spirit? What is our brand-new cart? Is it a "little image?" A bit more acceptance from our peers?

We need to listen up with ears to hear, and we need to live it up with the Holy Spirit. What do I mean by "live it up with the Holy Spirit?" If you read the whole of Galatians 5, you'll see Paul's teaching about the difference between living "according to the flesh" and "living according to the Spirit." He says those who live in the Spirit walk with the Spirit. Then he says, "keep in step with the Spirit." You'll notice Paul keeps saying things over and over again as if he is desperate for us to understand. He recognized there is something unique that needs to happen here. We need to look at our own lives to get in pace with God. Because if we will walk where He walks and we will live as He lives and we will keep pace with Him, then suddenly, all these other things grow in our lives. Things like love, joy, peace, patience, kindness, goodness, faithfulness, gentleness, and self-control. Those are the Fruits of the Spirit.

When we're in step with and walk in and with the Spirit, it produces something excellent in our lives. What many of us wish for regarding the Fruits of the Spirit is to go to God's grocery store and buy everything we need to add to our lives—like ingredients for a recipe. We want the easy button. But God said *it's fruit.* To get the best, you've got to *grow it in your lives.* The store-bought kind lacks the genuine flavor.

The only way you grow fruit is through acts of intimacy with the Holy Spirit. The first act is when the seed goes into the ground and it begins to take in the nutrients from the soil. The soil feeds the seed and waters it. Jesus said the seed dies to come to life. It begins to grow and break through the ground. And when those leaves start coming out, photosynthesis takes place from the sunlight and the air. The new plant continues to take things into its system. It never stops the act of intimacy it has below the surface, within the root system. There are two acts of intimacy going on at the same time, one above and one below the ground. When the plant gets large enough, it produces its first flower. The third act of intimacy begins while the first two acts continue happening. The birds and bees get involved through pollination. Intimacy builds on intimacy to produce the fruits of love, joy, peace, patience, kindness, goodness, gentleness, faithfulness, and self-control.

When you walk with and keep pace with the Spirit, you can't buy those things. You can't just add those things to your life. You must grow those things. The steps of a righteous person are ordered by the Lord. And you have the pace. Keep in step with the spirit.

I believe God is going to take us to places that we don't even know yet in our journeys to Next. I believe God is going to do things that are immeasurably more than all we could ask or imagine (Ephesians 3:20). I believe He is he's going to do all this with people who are ready for it. He's going to do these things with people who have put on the right shoes of expectation.

Get ready for a new pace; we are going to be stepping with the Holy Spirit!

PRAYER

God, I pray in the name of Jesus for everyone who is reading this chapter, that they would put on the shoes of expectation. The shoes that will enable them to find the pace You are setting for them. I pray that every one of us will be in a place where

we can hear what the Spirit is saying—have ears to hear—
because the Spirit is giving us the cadence we need to do so.
The Spirit is going to reveal the path and line us up, Lord. The
Spirit is going to give us the pace to follow. The Spirit will
empower us so that we stay engaged and move forward for
Your Kingdom. And I thank You, Lord, for what you're about
to do in our lives.

8

THIS PROCESS MIGHT SURPRISE US

The Next journey requires an availability to His process.

E ven if the Lord determines our paths and sets our pace, we have to keep in step. Remember, those words, *in step,* in the Greek form a military term that means to be in line, in order, and on pace. There is a process we need to work through to be on the right path and at the right pace.

PROCESS: RENEW

If you are going to start a new exercise program this year, one option is to walk. Or you might decide to jog. There are groups that advertise training programs where you can train to run a marathon a year from the time you start the program. In case you didn't know, a marathon is a 26.2-mile run. These programs train you gradually throughout the year to build your capacity to run an entire marathon. (To be clear; I am not selling anything, though I would suggest if you do choose to run a marathon for the first time, you chose one that happens on flat land and in a warmer climate—but not too warm.)

I have personal goals that include walking and running for certain distances. Sometimes, I reach my goals, and sometimes, I do not. When I lived in Florida, I walked and ran in that warmer climate on the flat land. When I moved to the Atlanta area, it was not flat anymore. I had not run hills since I had been a teenager. Let's just say that was a long time ago. I do try to stay in shape, but if I'm going to start something new, like running up hills, there are things I need to know. There are things you'd need to know too. We need to eat better. We need to stretch more. We need to prepare ourselves for the differences. It doesn't work to just go to the gym and work out with heavy weights and immediately jump into long distances. If you do that, you are going to hurt yourself in places you did not know existed—or so I have heard. If we take the time to prepare ourselves and create a safe and reasonable pace to improve, we can get to where we want to be.

It is the same with finding our path and pace with the Spirit. We have got to learn that we may need to stretch to do what God has for us because we may be at a pace we are not used to. If I am going to start running with Jesus, then I do not want to pull any muscles and miss any time with Him.

Once I rode in a 500-mile mission-based fundraiser, a bike-a-thon if you will. You read that correctly—a hundred miles a day for five days in a row with about thirty other people. I thought I was well prepared after training for six months prior to race day. However, on the first day, in those first one hundred miles, we rode into a twenty-mile-per-hour headwind. I found out I was not prepared for that. In fact, in full disclosure, I was trying to figure out which injury I could fake so I would not have to do any more of the one-hundred-mile days. I had a little pride; I wanted the injury to appear to be real. I finally decided I would "pull my quad" since most people don't know much about the quad. It's the big muscle group on the front side and the top half of your leg. It's hard to check a quad to determine if it's injured. Do you know what I'm saying? Nobody would know if I was fooling them or not. So I was ready to fake my injury when I went out the next morning. But that pride thing gripped me again, and I could not do it. I stretched a lot (and applied a lot of Icy Hot balm). In fact, at every stop that day, I stretched even more. I stretched through all of my pain and discomfort, and I finished the next hundred miles. Then, I finished the whole 500-mile bike ride.

STRETCHING: HOW WINESKINS ARE LIKE US

To find our Next's God-inspired new pace and path, we have to stretch through all of our challenges, pain, and discomforts. Jesus talks about this too. Jesus talks about how when he wants to do something new in you, there is a stretching process. Look at this passage in Luke 5:33: "One day some people said to Jesus, 'John the Baptist's disciples fast and pray regularly, and so do the disciples of the Pharisees. Why are your disciples always eating and drinking?' Jesus responded, 'Do wedding guests fast while celebrating with the groom? Of course not. But someday the groom will be taken away from them, and then they will fast.'"

Let me pause this story for a moment and interject this thought: *Someday.* We are living in the "someday" Jesus referred to. Jesus, the groom, is not here physically, in human form, like he was then. He has left and ascended to the Father in Heaven. In this "someday," we should pray and fast. That's what Jesus taught. In verse 36, we continue as Jesus gave them this illustration: "No one tears a piece of cloth from a new garment and uses it to patch an old garment. For then, the new garment would be ruined, and the new patch wouldn't even match the old garment."

A patched garment would have a fresh look and a new pattern or texture.

Jesus didn't stop with the garment illustration. He went on with another illustration: no one puts new wine into old wineskins because the new wine will burst the old wineskins, spilling the wine and ruining the skins. Old wineskin is usually hard leather. It's crusty because it's been around. It's not as flexible. Basically, there is no elasticity.

New wine must be stored in new wineskins. New wineskins are made with new leather. New leather is pliable. It has elasticity, it's soft. There is more room for new wineskin to be filled. That's an important part.

What we don't think about regarding the old wineskin is that it is experienced. With experience comes wisdom—or, at least, it should. That wineskin has been tested and has shown success. In looking at our experience in the Church, there are a lot of wise people; though, some just call them old. Wineskins aren't offended by that thought (they're inanimate!), but some people can get offended.

Look at what Jesus said in the last sentence of the passage when he talks about this. In essence, he said, "Everybody wants the old wine." Now, I'm not a wine drinker, but those who are wine drinkers, tell me: isn't there truth to the saying the older the wine is, the better it is? So everybody *does* want the old wine. Nobody wants the new wine when it's first made. Right?

Here's what the challenge is with the old wineskins in the Church: we may not understand what to do with the old wineskins. All the wine is gone. So what do you do with an old wineskin that has great experience and great wisdom? Remember, we can't put new wine in the old skin because when it ferments, it will burst and destroy the old skin. This old wineskin can't handle the new wine. It's already been stretched once. It can't handle it again, Jesus says. When the wineskin burst, it's no good for anything anymore.

It's okay to lose the old wine out of the old wineskin. But all the growth and development leaves with it. If we are looking for growth on a new path, with a new pace, then wisdom and experience are great commodities to have on the journey. Often, used old wineskins (a.k.a., people) are viewed as religious, traditional, inspirational, and wise with experience. They might be "religious" or more traditional. But they're typically inspirational and wise with experience.

If you're a wine drinker and I offered you old wine in an old wineskin or new wine in a new wineskin and said you could have whichever you want, you're going to come get the old out of the old because it's better. The old wineskin has learned from yesterday's revelation and has become today's wisdom.

But remember, old, wise wineskins won't grow anymore. Growth requires that we take in new wine and new revelation. Seems to me we need both.

BE SUBMERGED IN THE WORD

Let's look at Ezekiel 36:25–28: "Then I will sprinkle clean water on you, and you will be clean. Your filth will be washed away, and you will no longer worship idols. **And I will give you a new heart, and I will put a new spirit in you. I will take out your stony, stubborn heart and give you a tender, responsive heart. And I will put my Spirit in you** so that you will follow my decrees and be careful to obey my regulations. And you will live in Israel, the land I gave your ancestors long ago. You will be my people, and I will be your God" (bold emphasis mine).

We must get the old, stony heart out. We must let God move, allow Him to put a tender, responsive heart in us. This also makes room for the Spirit. In light of this passage, we've got to get rid of our old wineskin to put in the new wineskin, to be able to take in new wine (love) and new revelation (His Word).

So what do we do? How do we just throw out and discard everybody who's been in church for any length of time, the stony hearts or the old skins? If you feel like you're one of these old wineskins, that you've taken in wine, developed, grown, and stretched, but now you're stagnant—unsure how to keep growing past those old, hard skins—I'm about to help. As an old wineskin, you have another option. Some scholars say the Greek word for new wineskin can also be translated as *renewed* wineskin.

Wait, what? You mean to tell me there is a way to renew a wineskin? Absolutely!

Most wineskins in Jesus's day would have been made of goatskin. The skin would have been stretched and prepared and then sewn together. As these wineskins are sewn together, they put a bladder inside to hold the wine. Once it stretched through the fermenting process and after the wine was consumed, it became an empty, old wineskin. It may have been a wise old wineskin, but it was a wise, empty, old wineskin.

We have to get from wise, old, and empty wineskin to new again—to take in new revelation, thoughts, and ideas from the Spirit—new wine, if you will. If we're going to travel to our Next, at a new pace, we better have some plasticity, some pliability, and some flexibility. We better have the capacity for softness (gentleness). We better stretch a little more than we think we can because the spirit of God is going to grow us now.

Here is how the old wineskins were renewed: they would take the old wineskin once it was old and empty and submerge it, soaking it for days. After a period of time would pass, they would take it out of the water.

Water, in biblical terms, is renewal. We know water allows for washing. There is a cleansing that comes from the Lord. We know there is Living Water, the Word that makes us flexible. If you're not in the Word, my guess is you might be an old, wise, crusty, hard wineskin—one that is feeling a bit empty. But if you are in the Word, you're in the Living Water, and you get submerged with the Spirit of God.

Some people only hear the Word on Sunday mornings. If that's you, you're not submerging yourself in the Word. You're sticking your toe in. Ideally, you want to read the Word every day of your life. I believe—personally—you ought to be reading the Word all of the time. I believe you ought to read the Bible cover to cover every year. Yes, it is a big book. But did you know that if you spend about twelve to fifteen minutes a day reading, you can read the whole Bible in one year? I realize some believe they don't read very well or quickly. I'm glad you brought that up because in this day in time, electronic devices and programs will read the Word to you, and you can follow along. We live in a time when there is no excuse for not being submerged in the Word.

It's one thing for you to be in the Word. It's another thing for the Word to be in you. You can be in the Word, but you also want to get the Word in you.

The reason people used to submerge the old wineskin was to get every fiber of that leather to soften. If all you do is put it in the water and then take it out, it's going to get hard again. You put it in the water to soften it and recondition it. That's what your heart and soul need too.

The next step was to rub the wineskin with oil all through. It's for the same that baseball players oil their gloves—to maintain the soft, pliable characteristics over time. And we know in Scripture, oil is symbolic of the Holy Spirit.

We need to get in the Word; we need to get the Word in us; then, we need to allow the Holy Spirit to rub it deep into our lives, making us pliable—usable. The oil—or Spirit—helps us maintain the flexibility of our lives. We need to make room for the new wine (our Nexts) to be poured in by God.

NEW GENERATIONS OF NEXT

Is it worth it to travel through this entire process to receive new wine (become pliable and make room for Next)? God wants to stretch you for your Next. This new path and pace will take you to new destinies and destinations. This renewing process makes the journey better. In some cases, without the renewal, there will not be a journey— no Next—because we have to maintain that flexibility to follow God. Choose wisely, my brothers and sisters. Choose to be renewed.

One of Jesus's more famous quotes is when he said, "Get behind me Satan" (Matthew 16:23, Mark 8:33). He was addressing Peter directly as Peter and the other disciples were boldly proclaiming they would stand with Jesus as He stood facing those who wanted to take His life. Jesus was telling his disciples the time when they would be coming for him was soon. Most cannot quote the rest of what Jesus said in those passages. He started with, *Get away from me Satan*, then he continued with, "You are seeing things from a human point of view, not from God's."

This can be the difference between being an old wineskin and a new wineskin. The old wineskin had revelations that became wisdom, but due to the nature of old wineskins, is now not in the position to receive fresh revelation from God. The old wineskin has a point of view that is good, noble, and even wise, but it is not fresh, pliable, or flexible.

With new generations, we need new wine to reach them. Jesus himself represented new wine as He expanded the perception of the people of God to include the Gentiles, or non-Jews. The Holy Spirit represents new wine as Jesus ascended to Heaven and sent God's Spirit to empower every follower of Christ. Prior to the Holy Spirit coming to dwell in the life of every follower, God would manifest Himself, one entity at a time. Now, He manifests Himself through the work of the Holy Spirit in the life of every follower. He never leaves us or forsakes us. This may be the devil's worst nightmare. But to keep fighting the battle, new generations need us (the old wineskins) to be renewed, filled with new wine. Let's *go*!

PRAYER

God, take away the crusty, hard places in our lives. Take away our stony hearts and replace them with tender, receptive, responsive hearts. Take us through the process to renew us, submerge us in your Word, saturate us with your oil, and fill us with the new wine. May we receive a fresh Word, a fresh revelation, and a fresh faith that puts us on the pace and paths you have for us toward our Nexts.

9

DIVINE PURPOSE COMES WITH DIVINE PERSPECTIVE

We are a treasure carrier on the path and pace to Next.

A ll of us can be in step with the Holy Spirit, both in the path and at the pace He has for us. If we buck the process and get ahead, He has to reel us back in. If we get behind, He has to try to bring us ahead. If we're at pace with Him, God can do everything He wants to do in and through our lives. Now, part of this call is to **renew the perspective of our purpose**.

So, now we want to dive into 2 Corinthians 4:

> *Therefore, since God in his mercy has given us this new way, we never give up. We reject all shameful deeds and underhanded methods. We don't try to trick anyone or distort the word of God. We tell the truth before God, and all who are honest know this. If the Good News we preach is hidden behind a veil, it is hidden only from people who are perishing. Satan, who is the god of this world, has blinded the minds of those who don't believe. They are unable to see the glorious light of the Good News. They don't understand this message about the glory of Christ, who is the exact likeness of God. You see, we don't go around preaching about ourselves. We preach that Jesus Christ is Lord, and we ourselves are your servants for Jesus' sake. For God, who said, "Let there be light in the darkness," has made this light shine in our hearts so we could know the glory of God that is seen in the face of Jesus Christ. We now have this light shining in our hearts, but we ourselves are like fragile clay jars containing this great treasure. This makes it clear that our great power is from God, not from ourselves. We are pressed on every side by troubles, but we are not crushed. We are perplexed, but not driven to despair. We are hunted down, but never abandoned by God. We get knocked down, but we are not destroyed.*

Through suffering, our bodies continue to share in the death of Jesus so that the life of Jesus may also be seen in our bodies. Yes, we live under constant danger of death because we serve Jesus, so that the life of Jesus will be evident in our dying bodies. So we live in the face of death, but this has resulted in eternal life for you.

In my opinion, this is one of the most powerful passages in Scripture. God amazingly anoints Paul to write these words. I want to provide some insight into verse 7—regarding treasures in jars of clay. I want you to understand a couple of things. First, the jars of clay that Paul refers to are us.

Let's back up to Genesis where we see that God created Adam and Eve out of the dirt. Thus, we all are made from the same original ingredient: dirt. I guess we could say we are all just bags of dirt, right? Don't be offended by it. That's what we're made of! It reveals the incredible creativity of God to take dirt and a little moisture, whether it was spit or whatever liquid He used to make the mud, and fashion our human bodies.

Do you know the human body has eleven systems in it? All intricately working together? It is my understanding that if you take any of the systems completely out of the body, the rest cannot function, and you will die. God made all eleven systems with dirt: the integumentary system—or skin system that protects us—the skeletal system, the muscular system, the lymphatic system, the respiratory system, the digestive system, the nervous system, the endocrine system, the cardiovascular system, the urinary system, and the reproductive system. We cannot function well without any of these systems working properly in our bodies. Isn't God so amazing? To make all this from dirt and moisture? No scientist can make or create this kind of amazing masterpiece. God is the only one that can do it—and out of dirt!

Yet we function, no matter how intricate we are, just like jars of clay. This is what He said in Paul's letter to the Corinthian Church. There would be treasures in jars of clay.

In the period and culture this letter was written, if you had gold or silver or rubies or diamonds or some type of treasure, you would have found a place to store or hide it. They didn't have safes as we do now. They didn't have banks like we have today. So people would find a place to hide valuables in their homes or tents. Often, they would take their treasure and put it in a jar of clay. Why? Because if a thief is going to rob a house or tent, they are not likely going to look for treasures in everyday, common earthen vessels.

I know What I expect to find in a clay jar is some garbage or some leftover food, at best, or some seed or dirt. Maybe water. Maybe a plant. But I'd never expect to find treasure in a big clay jar. So as an ingenious idea, Paul uses that phrase for us to understand who we are. We're nothing more than dirt and moisture—jars of clay. Yet he declares there is a great treasure that could be inside each of us. The treasure Paul writes about is the gospel message. It is everything Jesus is to us, stored in our jars of clay. Isn't that amazing? God would take all that He is in his message, his gospel message, and store it inside us. Unholy, unrighteous, and challenged as we are, God does that. He puts the treasure of Himself inside us.

Paul had an expectation that people shouldn't hide their treasures but put them on display. He expected you to have treasure in your clay jars, but he never expected you to hide the treasure. He expected you to display God's power for all to see.

Let me show you what I'm talking about. Look at when He said: "We now have this light shining in our hearts, but we ourselves are like fragile clay jars containing this great treasure. This makes it clear that our great power is from God, not from ourselves" (2 Corinthians 4:7). In other words, everybody would have seen the display of this treasure, this gospel message, this great power. He wanted to make sure they knew that the great power people saw was not something the clay jar could do. It would leave no doubt that this power or treasure was something God was doing *through* them. God is on display *through us*. In this Scripture, there's a stated expectation that each of us would have a treasure that would be on display for other people around us to see.

Here is what we often do: We often get Jesus, the treasure, in our lives, our clay jars, and then we cover him up. We hide him, and we don't share him with anybody else. We keep others from seeing the powerful treasure of Jesus in our lives, the power that can give onlookers eternal hope and even the help they might need.

Paul wrote in the First Letter to the Corinthians that he wanted to be on display as a demonstration of the Spirit's power. I don't know if there is anybody in the New Testament that would have had a greater knowledge base and understanding and wisdom than Paul. Paul would have had the education level of a PhD. He could communicate in incredible ways. He could debate and never lose. Here is what Paul said of his own communication. In 1 Corinthians 2:3 (bold mine): "For I resolved to know nothing while I was with you except Jesus Christ and him crucified. I came to you in weakness with great fear and trembling. My message and my preaching **were not with wise and persuasive words, but with a demonstration of the Spirit's power**, so that your faith might not rest on human wisdom, but on God's power."

If anybody could have used his wise and persuasive words, Paul was the guy. He could go to the temple and debate and win. It wasn't about just his education. It wasn't about just his talent. It wasn't about just his abilities, and it wasn't about just his wise words. It was that he would be a demonstration of the Spirit's power. The purpose of this demonstration was so that man's faith might not rest on human wisdom but on God's power. It is not about how talented we are. It's not about how well we can do things. It's not about how great we are. It is about how great the gospel message is inside of us. It's about how great Jesus is. It's about how great the power of God is to change a life and that we *get to* be put on display as these fragile, cracked jars of clay.

If we are not careful, our talents, abilities, and words can hide rather than display our Jesus treasure. The only reason we have talent, ability, and skill is to display the gospel message of Jesus Christ. We may have lost this perspective.

WHEN CHALLENGES COME

Paul certainly would tell us that when you put something on display, **there are always challenges.** There will always be people who have something to say about our display or clay. There will be somebody who believes they can display it better, or at least differently.

Paul had challenges too. Here are the challenges Paul faced while displaying God's power. He said, "We are pressed on every side by troubles . . . perplexed . . . hunted down . . . knocked down . . . Through suffering, our bodies continue to share in the death . . . we live under constant danger of death . . . we live in the face of death" (2 Corinthians 4:7–12). Paul illuminated for us eight challenges he faced while displaying the grace and the message of the gospel of Jesus Christ.

Usually, our challenges tend to be selfish. Our challenges tend to be puny compared to what Paul listed. We often say things like, "I just can't do it because I'm not a very good talker." They are excuses. God does not call everybody to be a preacher or an evangelist. He just calls us to be on display, to communicate the treasure of His Good News.

How do I know that? Because he gave each of us a clay jar with a tongue and some lips and some vocal cords and a throat and another system that gets air through it all so we can display our treasure. There is no reason we cannot put on display the power or goodness of God. We have lost perspective when we've allowed these challenges to keep us from displaying the treasure and power of Jesus. If there was ever a time in our current history that the redeemed of the Lord should say something, it is now. Somebody, everybody, anybody should be displaying the treasure of Jesus and His power.

What a time for us to share. What a time for us to be a demonstration of the Spirit's power. The challenges Paul faced served as a backdrop that would allow the treasure to be seen very well. We, as the jars of clay, in the times we live, serve as a backdrop for the treasure of Jesus and His power to be seen by every onlooker, every person passing by, and everyone we intentionally encounter. I have no doubt that if we put diamonds, rubies, silver, or gold in a simple clay pot, everyone is going to see those things very well. Just like that, Paul said they would recognize the power is not from me. Rather, the treasure is inside me.

CHALLENGES BUILD RESOLVE

Resolve is the ability to do something when things are not easy. Paul just listed all those things that were difficult. When we display the treasure of God in our lives, when we exhibit the gospel, we must have resolve. And the resolve looks like this: We never give up.

Paul was saying to never give up on the call of Jesus to display the treasure that's inside of us.

Check out verses 15 and 16 in 2 Corinthians:

> *All of this is for your benefit. And as God's grace reaches more and more people, there will be great thanksgiving, and God will receive more and more glory. That is why we never give up. Though our bodies are dying, our spirits are being renewed every day.*

Do you know what happens when we never give up? It does not mean we won't be pressed on every side, perplexed, hunted down, knocked down, suffer, share in his death, be in constant danger, or live in the face of death. What it means to never give up is this:

> *When we are pressed on every side by troubles, we are not crushed; when we are perplexed, we are not driven to despair; when we are hunted down, we are never abandoned by God; when we get knocked down, we are not destroyed; when we are suffering, and our bodies continue to share in the death of Jesus so that the life of Jesus may also be seen in our bodies; when we live under constant danger of death because we serve Jesus, so that the life of Jesus will be evident in our dying bodies; and when we live in the face of death, this has results in eternal life for others.*

That's what happens when we don't give up. How do I know? Because when I haven't given up, I've found verse 16 comes into play: "That is why we never give up. Though our bodies are dying, our spirits are being renewed every day." Our bodies are dying as we face all those challenges. But our spirits are **renewed every day**.

If the only time we are renewed is on Sunday mornings, then we will not make it very long. We are going to wear out by Monday or Tuesday. There won't be much left to work with by Wednesday or Thursday. Our tanks will dwindle to nothing.

By Friday and Saturday, we will not make good choices. We are going to go out to places we should not go. We are going to make choices we should not make because we were not renewed every day. If the only time you feel renewed is that one day of the week, and then you will feel and be weak.

We have devices everywhere: phones, tablets, computers, and more. On most of our devices, there is an icon that indicates the amount of battery power left at any moment. It may be the device only has 25 percent power until you have to plug it in to charge it up. If we do not plug it in every day—usually at least once a day—then by the end of the day, the device will tick down to 20 percent, 10 percent, 2 percent, and finally, before 0 percent, we have a blank screen. We cannot use the device without renewing the power. Our lives are the same way. If we do not get plugged in to get renewed every day, we run out of power. By the end of every day, we are not going to have anything left to put God on display, nothing for His glory to be seen.

How do we plug into His power and renew every day? We pray. We get in His Word to get His Word in us. We meditate on the good things of God. We worship Him. Then our batteries get recharged. If our days are full of challenges and our batteries lose power quickly, we must create time to get back to Jesus. We must plug in a little more to get filled up a little more.

The reason we may not display His glory very well through our fragile clay jars is that our light is dim, dull, or diminished. The power has been used up. We must be recharged again and again every day. We must be renewed every day. One of the ways we can fill up with a sustainable power resource is with seasons of fasting and prayer. Therefore, I engage in seasons of prayer throughout each year.

As we resolve to display God's glory, it takes focus in our present troubles. Verse 17 says, "Our present troubles are small and won't last very long. Yet they produce for us a glory that vastly outweighs them and will last forever." It's the glory that lasts forever, not the troubles.

Look at verse 18. "So we don't look at the troubles we can see now . . ." God forgives us because we, as the Church, have come to a place where we focus more on the troubles than we do on the Glory. We focus more on the problems than we do on the person of Jesus. We may want to play back a recording of our prayer times. We'll come to the place where we'll say, "Oh God, I got this trouble, and I got this problem, and this is terrible. God, these things are happening. And that wife, you gave me. . . . Jesus, that husband you gave me, Lord. . . . . And those children you gave me." Too often, we talk about how bad our lives seem. It's time to quit telling God how annoying our problems are and tell our problems how big our God is. It's hard to do that when we're not focused on the right things.

Part of our resolve comes with knowing we're going to struggle along our journeys of Next. Jesus was clear about this. I hope these words set somebody free right now. Jesus warned us we're going to have troubles and having troubles won't be a temporary thing. Troubles are going to be part of our lives. That's just life. In fact, the Bible says, all our troubles will get worse in the end times. I know that's not shouting material, but that's the truth.

Our troubles produce for us a glory that far outweighs them and will last forever! So we don't look at the troubles. Rather, we *fix our gaze on the things that cannot be seen*. In other words, we must get our eyes off of our problems and get our eyes on the person of Jesus. He is the author, and the perfecter of our faith (Hebrews 12:2). Get your eyes off our culture and all that's going on with it. This doesn't mean we're not engaged. It doesn't mean we don't pray or give up. And it doesn't mean we stop representing Jesus in our culture. We just don't let our struggles, or our culture, get bigger than our Savior. And we let our Savior empower us to be who God has called us to be.

Don't allow your troubles to crowd out your purpose and perspective. Remember, Jesus said, "Do not let your hearts be troubled," and "In this world you will have trouble. But take heart! I have overcome the world" (John 14:1, 16:33).

We fix our attention on the things we cannot see because what we can see now will soon be gone. When do I mean? I know this may not be an encouraging word. But . . . we're all going to die. The problem is we don't think that is very encouraging. Yet Paul and other writers in the New Testament and Old Testament do. They talked about the fact we are going to die as a good thing because it means we're going to our eternal home. But we don't want to talk about death. I suppose because we don't like it. We, even in Christian circles, think of death as the end. However, death is a graduation ceremony for eternity with Jesus. We're not done. Our lives are not truly over. We're eternal creatures with spiritual dimensions. The question is *where* are we going to spend eternity (life after death). Yes, our bodies may be buried or burned, but we (our spirits) are long gone before then. We have a forwarding address. Hopefully, it's Heaven.

WRAPPING UP OUR PURPOSE

When we have this renewed perspective of our purpose, it changes everything. Let me help you. I don't know if you saw or read verse 12, but you must hear it now because it's the truth. Really, it is the foundation for everything else. Paul focuses on a renewed perspective of purpose. Verse 12 says, "So we live in the face of death, but this has resulted in eternal life for you."

We, as the Church, have been caught up, more expressed in the last few years, with our eyes on too many other things. If we dial in for preaching and teaching online or on the television or radio, we hear the "how to" for improving our lives on this earth. *How to live life now.* How to make your portfolio bigger in Jesus's name. How to be a success in this world. I'm not saying any of those goals are wrong in and of themselves. There may even be a good place for them somewhere. But if those goals are all there is, we've lost perspective. We have set ourselves up to live for the now when Jesus died for us to live forever. We're missing our Next purpose.

This perspective has to shift. It has to change. There has to be an eternal perspective in everything we do. When there is an eternal perspective, it changes everything. When we face our problems, we see them in the light of eternity. That's why Paul said he didn't even look at his troubles anymore. He just looked at what couldn't be seen. Why? Because he saw things in the light of eternity.

Therefore, when our treasure is put in our jars of clay, we're not concerned about our jar as much as we are about the treasure being seen.

Let's back up a wee bit to verse 15 to drive this home: "All of this is for your benefit. And as God's grace reaches more and more people, there will be great thanksgiving, and God will receive more and more glory." Now listen, the display of the treasure is for the redemption of mankind—for your family, your friends, your coworkers, your neighbors, and the people in your community. It is for all to come to Christ.

I want you to hear the next thing through the passion that dwells in my heart. We, as the Church, may have become more like the rest of the world than we want to admit. We've easily become more concerned about how many people have died from diseases or viruses like COVID-19 than whether they ended up in Heaven or Hell. Before you burn this book or send me an email telling me where to go, I want to be clear. I don't like it when people die of anything. As a pastor, I would suppose I deal with death and funerals more than the average person. During this pandemic, we have been living through, and with the influence of mass media, everyone is dealing with death in a more revealing way because it's in front of our eyes all of the time. I do not want you to die from any cause. However, I'm also a realist; we will all die. I am more concerned about where you are going to be after you die.

> I hope all Christ-followers will have a renewed perspective of their purpose, which, in part, is to display their glorious treasure (Jesus)—their redeemer, their hope, our Savior.

I know where I am going to be living forever. I've already sent the post office my forwarding address. When I die, just send my mail to the pearly gates of Heaven because that's where I'm going. The only way we can know where we are going through and after death is if we are in a personal relationship with Jesus.

Many people say things like, "God and me got something worked out, and he knows I want to go." What is that? Having something worked out ain't the deal with God. Jesus did not leave Heaven, live among us, be persecuted while He was here, die on the cross, be raised from the dead, ascend back to Heaven to pray for us, send the Holy Spirit to be our teacher and comforter, establish the Church, provide God's Word, and even call and send people to communicate His love to us so that we can have a "deal worked out" with Him. He expects a personal relationship with the total surrender of our lives to Him.

We, as followers of Christ, have been bought with a price; we are not our own. Without this understanding of a relationship with Him, our Next will not be from Him. We will believe we can repurpose our lives to accomplish what we are supposed to accomplish. Many people want to be in a relationship with Jesus as long as they are in control. Jesus does not offer that kind of deal. If you're going to be in a personal, surrendered relationship with Jesus, He's in control. He makes the choices. He has your Next.

THE ETERNAL PERSPECTIVE

The perspective has to shift. It has to be complete in nature and scope. It has to be eternal in every capacity. We see everything in light of eternity. We do everything in light of eternity. We are becoming eternal in nature. When we talk to our family, it should be with eternity in mind. When we spend time on the job, it should be with eternity in mind. When we go to the grocery store, it should be with eternity in mind.

We cannot be more concerned about whether we eat the right stuff or how we die than we are about whether people are going to Heaven and Hell. Jesus didn't die so that you could eat the right stuff. He didn't die so you wouldn't die, not in the physical sense. He died so that you could have eternity with Him. You and I can have an eternal shift with this eternal perspective.

I wasn't raised in church. So sometimes, I don't get it when people take truth and eternity for granted. I didn't experience growing up in a church where people took these things for granted. I never have and hope I never will. I never took for granted that my kids would be going to Heaven. Never. I talked to them and shared about Jesus from when they were little to now. They are adults now. I still talk to them about Jesus—about living a surrendered life. I never take anything related to eternity for granted, especially in lieu of my career as a pastor. If you are a leader or long-time member of the church I serve, I don't take for granted that you are going to Heaven. You can think I do not understand or appreciate the grace of God or the keeping power of God. Okay. When you get to Heaven, you will be glad about my passionate pursuit to get you on the right path, pace, process, and purpose—not just to your Next but to Heaven. For me, this is the compilation of having an eternal perspective.

Eternal purpose affects whether you display and how you display treasure. It affects your resolve. When you have an eternal perspective, the problems you face just will not matter as much anymore. Oh, they will still be there. They will still hurt. They will still be painful. But you recognize there is value in them. And part of the value is your spiritual and personal growth.

In fact, Paul said this to the Corinthian Church: I used to worry about my weaknesses, but now I don't even worry about my weaknesses. Now I look forward to my weaknesses because that is when God's power is made perfect (2 Corinthians 12:9). Paul looked forward to his weaknesses more than he did his strengths. That perspective flies in the face of our culture, our Western thought, because we all want to celebrate our strengths rather than our weaknesses.

When Paul said that about his weaknesses, he had prayed three times for something particular to be removed from his life, but God never removed it. This is when God said *I will make my power perfect in your weakness.* Paul replied with his

Next step response: *Check, got it. Let's move on. I'll live with this weakness my whole life, knowing I get to experience your power in the journey.*

Oh, that is a different response than what we usually hear, isn't it? We can fall into the mindset of thinking we only get His power and provision when everything is provided for us and all of our problems are gone. In other words—when everything is wonderful. When we experience health. When we received "great" blessings. We can easily believe those are the only times God has really blessed us. That is some bad theology, a bad understanding of a biblical presentation. That is certainly not what Paul taught.

Remember, Paul said:

> *We are pressed on every side by troubles, but we are not crushed. We are perplexed, but not driven to despair. We are hunted down, but never abandoned by God. We get knocked down, but we are not destroyed. Through suffering, our bodies continue to share in the death of Jesus so that the life of Jesus may also be seen in our bodies. Yes, we live under constant danger of death because we serve Jesus, so that the life of Jesus will be evident in our dying bodies. So we live in the face of death, but this has resulted in eternal life for you* (2 Corinthians 4:9–12).

I don't see anywhere in that passage where Paul says God is going to deliver him from any of these situations. It's just not there. I am not saying God can't remove our struggles. He is *able to* do "immeasurably more than all we ask or imagine" (Ephesians 3:20), but that does not mean he *is going to* do all we ask or imagine. Are you with me?

God can supply all of your needs according to His riches and glory. But that's not a promise that He is going to supply all of your needs when or how you want them. To be clear, God does not only work in poverty. He blesses in amazing ways. I am saying God works whether "you've got and are in plenty" or when "you don't got and are in need."

Paul also said he learned to be content in all situations, as in all of the time. Then he says the most famous part of the verse—the one athletes quote often, though they don't know the true contents. He said, "I can do all things through Christ who strengthens me" (Philippians 4:13). What Paul was talking about was the financial condition of his life. He said sometimes he had plenty and sometimes, he had nothing, but he learned to be content in every situation because he can do all things through Christ.

It's time we have a perspective of our purpose shift to have eternity at the forefront.

PRAYER

Father, give us a shift in our perspective about our purpose; let us see everything in light of eternity. Change our focus. Change our resolve. Change how we display the treasure of God in our lives. I pray that we would recognize we are just clay jars with a treasured purpose inside of us, which the world needs to see and experience for themselves.

God, I pray that we would have a shift in our perspective, our eternity—that we will view eternity in everything we see and do. Renew us, make us ready for the new wine, and fill us.

We are asking you to speak, Lord, for your servants are listening.

Now, take a moment to just meditate on Him. Learn to do this daily. Write down in your journal impressions or words that you believe God might be saying to you. Review these weekly and pray over them again. If you need more clarity, ask a spiritual mentor or leader to pray with you as you share your thoughts with them. This helps you to determine what God is saying, shifting, or directing in your journey to your Next.

10

NO NEXT WITHOUT YOU

Moses (was resolute and) said, "Now show me your glory"
(Exodus 33:18).

A s we have determined, God has our Nexts. And since this is true, then we should only move into our Nexts with His presence, His glory with us. His Presence and Glory are the empowering and keeping elements of our Nexts.

One of my favorite Old Testament passages is found in Exodus 33:14. This, again, is about Moses, one of my favorite guys. One of the first things Moses did in leadership for the Israelites was mess up. Maybe that's why I like Moses so much—because he made mistakes and he made comebacks. He may be the comeback king.

If you recall, Moses was on the edge of moving forward to lead the people of Israel to the Promised Land. Then God said (in my own words), You know, I kind of have had enough, and I am not going to move forward with you. I will send you, but I am not personally going with you. You can just go do your thing. I am for you and will send you, but I am not going with you, Moses.

That is that moment in Exodus 33, "Then the LORD said to Moses, "Leave this place, you and the people you brought up out of Egypt, and go up to the land I promised on oath to Abraham, Isaac and Jacob, saying, 'I will give it to your descendants.' I will send an angel before you and drive out the Canaanites, Amorites, Hittites, Perizzites, Hivites and Jebusites. Go up to the land flowing with milk and honey. **But I will not go with you**, because you are a stiff-necked people and I might destroy you on the way" (verses 1–3, emphasis mine).

This was disconcerting news for Moses and the people of Israel. I imagine for Moses, it was a serious issue because he had to be with all of the Israelites without God there to help him navigate dealing with the nearly million former Egyptian slaves that, at some point, wanted to kill Moses and return to Egypt. Maybe for the Israelites, it was an issue because they would be going somewhere they had never been, living somewhere they had never lived, and the only leader they had was someone with a reputation of not handling conflict so well (after all, he killed a guy while trying to resolve a conflict).

Maybe it is disconcerting news because God is clear: "But I will not go with you." God is straightforward. I'm sure the people wondered, "So do we take our chances with Moses or God or go back to Pharoah?"

The following verses reveal the initial responses of the Israelites:

> *When the people heard these distressing words, they began to mourn and no one put on any ornaments. For the Lord had said to Moses, "Tell the Israelites, 'You are a stiff-necked people. If I were to go with you even for a moment, I might destroy you. Now take off your ornaments and I will decide what to do with you.'" So the Israelites stripped off their ornaments at Mount Horeb* (Exodus 33:5–6).

God gives room for other options with the statement, "and I will decide what to do with you." He commanded the Israelites to *take off your ornaments,* and they did. This was a call to humility and repentance. Their response was critical regarding God deciding whether He would go with them. Those ornaments were jewelry or decorations they would commonly wear. I might suggest those ornaments came from Egypt, for they had not been too long gone from Egypt, and we do not have a record of them taking a shopping trip to a local mall in the desert to buy new ornaments. Thus, my suggestion is this:

these ornaments kept them connected to their identity in Egypt and to their former slavery. These ornaments could have served as a reminder that they belonged to Pharoah. God needed them to see themselves as no longer belonging to Egypt or Pharoah, but now free to be in a relationship with and follow Him.

Sometimes, we have "ornaments" in our lives or ministries that connect us to our pasts—or even our present—making it difficult for us to move into a new season, a new identity . . . into our Next. God may ask us to lay these ornaments aside and move with Him.

Personally, I keep awards or recognitions in containers and not on display. I do this because I don't want to be distracted by the accomplishments of my past. I want to move forward to every Next God has for me rather than living in the last Next. I can appreciate, learn from, and build upon my past successes and failures. I just do not want to live in them. I want to live for my next.

Listen in to Moses as he prays in the tent of meeting— his special meeting place with God: "Moses said to the LORD, 'You have been telling me, 'Lead these people,' but you have not **let me know whom you will send with me.** You have said, 'I know you by name and you have found favor with me.' If you are pleased with me, teach me your ways so I may know you and continue to find favor with you. **Remember that this nation is your people**" (Exodus 33:12, NIV, emphasis mine).

Notice Moses acknowledged that God may not go with him: *let me know whom you will send with me.* He also asked God for continued instruction, growth, and favored help.

Then, Moses reminds God, *Remember that this nation is your people*. This statement may be the part of the prayer that influences the decision God will make. I hear two things being said. The first one is that Moses reminded God that he will answer God's call to lead these people. Moses was related to them, but his leadership came with humility—he did not own them. He owned his leadership calling. The second thing I hear is that Moses reminded God that these were His people. In other words, God is responsible for them. Moses came boldly yet humbly before the throne of Grace.

Here is how the rest of the prayer session went (Exodus 33:14–18, NIV):

> *The Lord replied, "My Presence will go with you, and I will give you rest."*

> *Then Moses said to him, "If your Presence does not go with us, do not send us up from here. 16 How will anyone know that you are pleased with me and with your people unless you go with us? What else will distinguish me and your people from all the other people on the face of the earth?"*

> *And the Lord said to Moses, "I will do the very thing you have asked, because I am pleased with you and I know you by name."*

> *Then Moses said, "Now show me your glory."*

Moses said, unless you go with us, distinguish me and your people from all the other people on the face of the earth. And the Lord said to Moses, I will do the very thing you have asked, because I am pleased with you and I know you by name. Moses knew moving forward to their Next, he needed some identity that would be unquestionable. Here is a great ministry leadership lesson. We need His identity more than we need any other. We need His identity more than we need a celebrity or influencer, a great social media following, a denominational recognition, or something else. This identity in Him is built in relationship; remember, God said *and I know you by name.*

This leads to one of the shorter prayers in the Bible. It may be one of the most powerful prayers in the Bible. Moses said, "Now show me your glory" (Exodus 33:18). When we can understand the value of this short prayer, we will want to pray this consistently as we journey to, arrive at, and live out our Next.

Remember what Paul said in 2 Corinthians 3:18: "So all of us who have had that veil removed can see and reflect the glory of the Lord. And the Lord—who is the Spirit—makes us more and more like him as we are changed into his glorious image." We are all called to see and reflect the glory of the Lord. To be clear, His glory is considered His manifest presence in our lives. Remember, God is a Spirit at work in our lives. We live in a physical human realm or dimension. We also have our human spirit with which we learn to connect with God's Spirit. It takes faith, recognition, time, and engagement to connect with God spiritually. We will also have to take off ornaments and remove veils to connect at deeper levels with God. As we connect in this way, we are made more and more like Him. We are being changed into His glorious image.

This knowledge of God's glory motivated Moses to pray, "Now show me your glory." We must have a recognition of what we need. If we do not know what we need, we may not go get it. Do you know what I am talking about? If the gas gauge on your car is broken, unless you're keeping up with the mileage, you may not know you need some gas until you are left alone on the road without a way to get some gas to your car. Had you known you needed gas, you could have filled up. It changes everything.

If we do not know what we need, we do not go get it. Moses had a recognition of what he needed. Moses had all the leadership skills. He had all the practical skills. Moses had the people with him. Having the people with him was not the goal. Moses got them out of Egypt. Getting them out of Egypt was not the goal. Moses was leading them to the Promised Land. Even getting them to the Promised Land was not the goal. Moses knew he had not arrived and knew he would not get there if the Lord was not with him. He knew he needed God's glory. That was the ultimate goal. And it should be ours too.

Need proof? Here is what he said: What else will distinguish me and your people from all the other people on the face of the earth (Exodus 33:16, paraphrased)? In other words, he knew that there would be nothing that would distinguish the Israelites from any other people, except God's glory. Moses knew the ultimate goal was the identity the people of Israel would have as the people of God, *marked by His glory*. He knew His glory would give them everything they would need: provision, protection, power, purpose, process, and even pace. He knew God's glory would give them and keep them in their Next, in Him.

Listen to me, friends and family. There's nothing that would distinguish us from all the other people in Atlanta (where I live), the USA, or the world, except God's glory. I'm not talking about just churches. I'm talking about people groups. There are a lot of great civic organizations. There are a lot of great groups that do a lot of great things, and the Church can do a lot of great things. But the only thing that makes us different—it's not what we do—is Who is with us. God's glory upon us. That is the only thing that makes us different from everybody else. **We need His glory revealed to us.**

PRESENCE OVER PERMISSION

Many people want His permission, not His presence. In other words, they want God to say something like, "Okay, go ahead. I'll let you do that." Then, they will do it. They will come back and report to the Lord. The Lord is not interested in just giving you permission. He is interested in you having His presence. When you want His presence, then all of a sudden, God can do amazing things in your life. When you have His presence, there is accountability. There is power. There is anointing. There is everything you would need for life and godliness.

We need God's glory to function in and through our lives every day. I grew up watching TV. I was a TV kid. (It was new at the time.)

We had this box in our house, a big brown box. They told everyone it was a piece of furniture with a screen in it, and our TV was in color. That was a big deal back in the late sixties and seventies. I would sit in front of the TV and watch a lot of it growing up. It was my babysitter in a lot of ways.

One of my favorite shows was the "Andy Griffith Show." Let me tell you why I liked "Andy Griffith" . . . because they were simple people. They were country, small-town people, much like where I grew up. I ate the food they like. I liked the hunting and fishing they did. I liked the games they played. I think you can get the picture.

Andy was the local sheriff. He was also the daddy to a son—a little red-headed kid named Opie. The mother figure was Aunt Bee. Andy did not have a wife. The first episode explained to viewers that his wife had died, and it was never mentioned again. Part of the comedy of the show was when Andy dated ladies, but he never re-married. Andy was always a single father raising Opie. These details play into under- standing this illustration.

There was a particular episode where Opie came up to his daddy with his little wagon. Opie had packed all of his stuff into his wagon. Andy asked Opie, "Where are you going?"

Opie said, "I'm running away now." Opie was four or five years old—a little cute little kid.

Andy said, "Wait a minute before you go." Andy ran upstairs and came back downstairs with a packed bag. Opie looked at him.

"What you doing?"

Andy said something like, "I'm going with you. You can run away. But I'm going with you." The episode ended with the two hugging one another and deciding not to run away.

I have told my wife several times over the years, especially when she would be aggravated with me because I aggravated her, "You can leave anytime you want to, but know this: I'm going with you."

It is that same tenacity that Moses had with the Father. When he said, "God, I'll go where you want me to go, but I ain't going by myself. I ain't talking to a million Israelites by myself. I ain't talking with my brother and my sister by myself. I am not leaving here without You," (yes, my southern slang gets in the mix when I paraphrase), Moses showed God that he recognized the truth that he couldn't accomplish what God wanted without God being there. That's when Moses was positioned for God to reveal His glory through his life.

> **We have to have a recognition of what we need—for God to reveal His glory in us—on the inside. It's called our treasure.**

Here's the ending to this part of the story. Moses asked, "' How will anyone know that you are pleased with me and with your people unless you go with us?' . . . And the LORD said to Moses, 'I will do the very thing you have asked, because I am pleased with you and I know you by name'" (Exodus 33:16–17). Now that is a powerful statement for the God of the universe to make about anybody. And He made it to Moses. Basically, He said, "because *I am pleased with you* and *I know you by name*."

VACANCY

You can go to any hotel in Atlanta. If you do, you will usually find on the sign somewhere out front, or in the front window or on the front of the building, that says either "vacancy" or "no vacancy." Vacancy means they have a room for you. If you can afford the room, you can stay there. No vacancy means they are sold out. There is no place for you to stay. We as individuals (and the Church as a family) need to get to a place where we have put up a vacancy sign for the Spirit of the living God. We need to make room for His glory to come deep into our lives and do what His glory does for us. We often put up a no vacancy sign because we try to do all He asks of us without Him. We cannot do it without Him. Moses knew this. We must have the same resolve and realization of who we are and hang out the vacancy sign for His glory as we pray, worship, and serve.

In his letter to the Corinthians, Paul said all of us who have had the veil removed can see and reflect the glory of the Lord. He is talking about the old covenant and the new covenant. The Old Covenant—the Old Testament, the law—and all its parts were a veil for the people. The old covenant was a veil that kept the people from experiencing the new covenant in Christ. If they were still trying to live by the old covenant, he said the old has to go, and the new has to come. The old covenant really had become more of a god to the people than the God of the old covenant was to them. In other words, the law became their god. The law, although it was intended to describe and develop their relationship with God, distracted the people from the relationship that God wanted with his people. We have to recognize who we are, who He is, and our vital need to be in a relationship to see and reflect His glory.

There are wonderful people who have a veil installed over their lives. They are living where their traditions, way of thinking, way of doing, and personal veils have caused them not to experience the glory of God. Paul said, when the veil is removed, we can see the glory of God. We can't see through the veil. The veil will keep us trapped from His glory.

The writer of Hebrews said this in Hebrews 12:14: "Make every effort to be holy without holiness no one will see the Lord." None of us will see the Lord if we do not have holiness in our lives. How can we expect a holy God to be a part of our lives if we are living in unholy ways? It may be in our attitude. It may be our mindset. It may be our spirit. It may be our behavior. When we live in unholy ways consistently and ignore the work of the Spirit of God in our lives, we cannot expect the Holy Spirit to dwell in an unholy vessel. You and I have to get to a place where there is a realization of who we are.

When the Spirit of God speaks to us, we should release the veils in our lives, which are keeping us from experiencing the glory of God. John—the Revelator, as he is called—wrote to seven churches, and those letters are recorded in Revelations 2–3. With the anointing of the Spirit, He wrote what Jesus spoke to each church. He ends each of the seven letters to the churches with the same phrase: "He who has an ear, let him hear" what the Spirit is saying to the church. That does not mean that the Spirit had not been speaking before. It means that they had not been listening. You and I may not be listening because the Spirit may be talking about our veils. We may think, I do not mind the Spirit moving and talking and doing, as long as He is not messing with me and my stuff. As long as He is not telling me what I need to do. As long as He is not telling me what I need to surrender. As long as He is not telling me what I need to give up. As long as He is not telling me what I need to change. When He gets all up in our business, we think this Word is for someone else. How can we expect the glory to be revealed to us if there is no room for the glory—if we've put up a "no vacancy" sign, and if we keep our veils on? Let us expect the glory to fall on us and in us.

GLORY THROUGH US

Once God's glory is revealed to us and then in us, we have made room for Him. Next, His glory wants to reflect through us. That's what Paul said. He said all of us who have had the veil removed can see and reflect the glory of the Lord. Listen to this statement.

> **We cannot reflect what we do not behold; We cannot behold what we cannot see, and we cannot see what is veiled from our view.**

We have considered two of those already. We know we cannot see what is veiled. The veil has to be removed for us to see His glory. We have considered that we cannot behold what we cannot see. We cannot take it in if there is stuff in the way in our lives.

Let's now consider the reflecting part. We can reflect what we have beheld. That terminology is the same terminology that you would find when discussing the use of a mirror. If we want to see ourselves when we get up in the morning, we pass by a mirror somewhere in our house to take a look. We all want to see how presentable we are or how much work we have to do to get ready for the day.

We look in the mirror because we want to see our image. We want to see if when we paid $200 for our hairstyle was worth it. We want to see if all that makeup we bought, that we were supposed to be able to sleep in, was worth it. We want to see if our designer outfits were worth it. We want to see if all the jewelry we hung on our bodies was worth it. If we move or remove ourselves from in front of the mirror, it cannot behold our image any longer. If I am on the backside of the mirror, the mirror cannot behold my image. If I am to the left or to the right of the mirror, the mirror cannot behold my image. It's only if I am in front of the mirror that the mirror will capture and behold my image. Most days, I think I hear my mirror saying, "Wow, that is a good-looking dude right there." My mirror says, "I am telling you, Jesus, you did good." The mirror says, "Boy, your wife has got good taste. Hallelujah." (Just to be transparent, I'm kidding. My mirror does not talk to me. I'm not losing my mind.)

Here is what the Bible says in the NKJV (emphasis mine): "But we all, with unveiled face, **beholding as in a mirror the**

glory of the Lord" (2 Corinthians 3:18). We can behold the glory of God as the mirror does our image.

We cannot behold the glory of God from anywhere, but right in His presence or face to face with Him. When we get in the presence of God, we can behold His image. We can behold His glory. When we get His glory beheld in us, His glory can then be displayed all around our world through us. Everybody can see His glory. His glory is not going to be seen through us when we are too far away from Him. The further we get away from Him, the further our image of His glory becomes, maybe even to be unrecognizable. To take in the glory of God, we have to be close—intimate. He makes this glory beholding available to every one of us. God, being Spirit, can make Himself available to all who follow Him, all around the world, at any given time, if we will only position ourselves for His glory, face to face with Him.

Why are we going to behold His glory? Why would Moses pray with such intentionality that God showed him His glory? Why would we want His glory if we are already on our way or have arrived at our Next? Peter reminds us. Peter says everything we need for life and godliness is in His manifest presence (2 Peter 1:3).

We are not going to get everything we need for our Next in this book. We are not going to get everything we need for our Next in our education. We are not going to get everything for our Next in strategies. Everything we need for finding our Next, moving to our Next, and, do not miss this, arriving and functioning in our Next is found in His glory, the divine manifest presence of His Holy Spirit. When you behold His glory, then you can reflect His glory. He is not looking for people who want permission. He's looking for people who want his Presence. What are you looking for?

Do you know what I need? I do not need anyone to remember my name. I do not need anybody to remember my face. I know that I am called as a follower of Christ to reflect His glory. I need them to see His face. When I speak or write, I need people to see and hear *His words*. I need them to feel His touch when I touch them. When I talk to them, when I am in their presence, I just want to reflect His glory.

What about you? What about your Next? God has got you. God has got your Next. Behold Him. Behold His glory!

Trust Him . . . and remember, don't let that quarter out-trust you as you pursue His Nexts for you.

ABOUT THE AUTHOR

Mike Tedder is a pastor in near Atlanta, Georgia. He has served in many ministry and leadership roles for over forty years. His greatest joys in ministry have been in serving as a youth pastor, lead pastor, and evangelist. His relational leadership and humor drive him to bring help and joy to all he encounters. He feels his greatest ministry is to his family: his wife, three kids, and their spouses, and, at this writing, six grandkids.

A free ebook edition is available with the purchase of this book.

To claim your free ebook edition:

1. Visit MorganJamesBOGO.com
2. Sign your name CLEARLY in the space
3. Complete the form and submit a photo of the entire copyright page
4. You or your friend can download the ebook to your preferred device

Morgan James BOGO™

A **FREE** ebook edition is available for you or a friend with the purchase of this print book.

CLEARLY SIGN YOUR NAME ABOVE

Instructions to claim your free ebook edition:
1. Visit MorganJamesBOGO.com
2. Sign your name CLEARLY in the space above
3. Complete the form and submit a photo of this entire page
4. You or your friend can download the ebook to your preferred device

Print & Digital Together Forever.

Snap a photo

Free ebook

Read anywhere